BALLET: BEYOND THE BASICS

BALLET :•

BEYOND THE BASICS

SANDRA NOLL HAMMOND

MAYFIELD PUBLISHING COMPANY

Copyright © 1982 by Mayfield Publishing Company
First edition 1982

All rights reserved. No portion of this book may be
reproduced in any form or by any means without
written permission of the publisher.

Library of Congress Catalog Card Number: 81-84696
International Standard Book Number: 0-87484-522-X

Manufactured in the United States of America

Mayfield Publishing Company
1280 Villa Street
Mountain View, CA 94041

Sponsoring editor: C. Lansing Hays
Manuscript editor: Carol Dondrea
Designer: Nancy Sears
Illustrator: Diana Thewlis
Cover illustrator: Diana Thewlis
Layout: Mary Wiley
Production manager: Cathy Wilkie
Compositor: Imperial Litho/Graphics
Printer and binder: George Banta Company

CONTENTS

CHAPTER SIX   LEARNING FROM HISTORY   127

PREFACE

This book is dedicated to those students who, having studied—if not yet completely mastered—ballet basics, find themselves in that in-between, "gray" area, no longer beginners, not yet advanced dancers. Catch-all labels—Intermediate, Continuing, Ballet II—attempt to categorize both participants and their technical level. At the very minimum, such terms imply certain attributes: familiarity with basic ballet terminology, understanding of correct body placement, and a general ease in performing elementary technique. Probably the students feel better, look better, at the barre than in center floor. Their technical capacities may include single *pirouettes* but not doubles, strong *changements* but not *entrechats quatre*.

A certain smugness has been earned—students can "speak ballet," they display considerable ballet paraphernalia, they can be as determined and proud as daily joggers—but also a certain vulnerability has crept in. The glow of the beginner has faded, the thrill of accomplishment may appear less frequently, technical plateaus and frustrations curse the studio and all occupants.

The phase is familiar to dancers the world over. It is one that must be lived through if ballet's benefits are to be realized—the very real pleasure of participation in a beautiful art form.

The aim of this book is to provide those "Intermediate" students a reference source for their expanded technical development and also suggestions for their artistic growth as dancers. In addition, the book offers ideas from ballet's technical past, a revival of some valuable elements from its rich tradition. Most especially, these chapters are meant as a loving encouragement to students and teachers who find themselves dealing with this most challenging phase of ballet training, the period beyond the basics.

THE CLASSROOM CONNECTION

All dancers can trace their ballet "roots" to some sort of "family tree," such as the one on the next page, which shows the training heritage of the great British ballerina Margot Fonteyn. The classroom connection may go even beyond Louis Dupré, famed dancer of the noble style at the Paris Opera, for he had worked with Louis Pécour, the celebrated choreographer of the late seventeenth and early eighteenth centuries. Unfortunately, little is known of Pécour's own life, although many examples of his compositions survive in notation.

Margot Fonteyn and Rudolf Nureyev in the pas de deux *from* Le Corsaire, *a ballet choreographed by Marius Petipa for the St. Petersburg Maryinsky Theatre in 1899. Earlier versions of the ballet were by Albert (London, 1837) and Mazilier (Paris, 1856). Photo: Houston Rogers.*

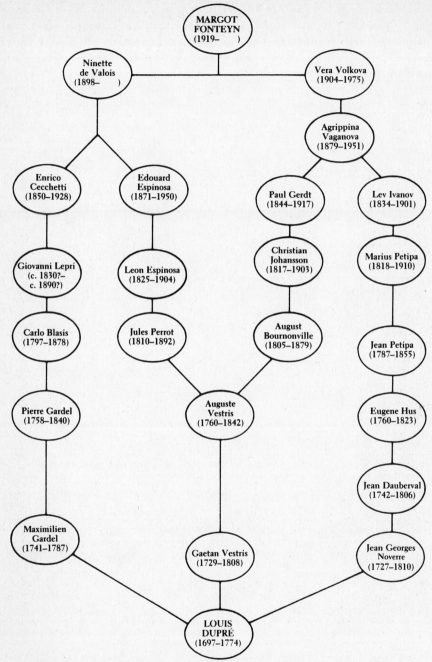

MARGOT
FONTEYN
(1919–   )

Ninette
de Valois
(1898–   )

Vera Volkova
(1904–1975)

Agrippina
Vaganova
(1879–1951)

Enrico
Cecchetti
(1850–1928)

Edouard
Espinosa
(1871–1950)

Paul Gerdt
(1844–1917)

Lev Ivanov
(1834–1901)

Giovanni Lepri
(c. 1830?–
c. 1890?)

Leon Espinosa
(1825–1904)

Christian
Johansson
(1817–1903)

Marius Petipa
(1818–1910)

Carlo Blasis
(1797–1878)

Jules Perrot
(1810–1892)

August
Bournonville
(1805–1879)

Jean Petipa
(1787–1855)

Pierre Gardel
(1758–1840)

Auguste
Vestris
(1760–1842)

Eugene Hus
(1760–1823)

Jean Dauberval
(1742–1806)

Maximilien
Gardel
(1741–1787)

Gaetan Vestris
(1729–1808)

Jean Georges
Noverre
(1727–1810)

LOUIS
DUPRÉ
(1697–1774)

Compiled by Lilian Moore, "The International Ballet Heritage," *Dance Magazine*, January, 1958. Reprinted in *Echoes of American Ballet*, a collection of articles by Moore (New York: Dance Horizons, 1976), p. 17.

**ACKNOWLEDG-
MENTS**

Illustrations for this book were made from photographs taken by G. Benton Johnson and Douglas Oliver of dancers Norrine Bessor, Katie Gill, Tamara Lohrenz, and Edward Rumberger. Special thanks also go to Julie McLeod and the Dance Warehouse of Santa Barbara for providing studio space for photography sessions and reconstruction of the historical material.

BALLET: BEYOND THE BASICS

George Zoritch, *internationally known* premier danseur noble, *danced leading roles with many major ballet companies, including the Ballet Russe de Monte Carlo and the Grand Ballet du Marquis de Cuevas, before beginning a teaching career in 1964. Like many of his distinguished professional colleagues, Zoritch later moved to a university dance program, joining the faculty of the University of Arizona in 1973. Photo: William Claxton.*

CHAPTER ONE
GETTING READY

It is in the classroom where we learn to dance and perform, not in the theatre. Seeing Galina Ulanova, the great Russian ballerina, taking class in her forty-ninth year was the greatest example of dedication, respect, and discipline I have ever witnessed in any classroom. No wonder this was reflected in her impeccably great artistic achievements.

George Zoritch, 1981.[1]

In a very important sense, a dancer never really leaves the classroom, for that is where the technique and art of ballet is learned, nurtured, and renewed. No matter how skilled or famous, a dancer continues to attend daily ballet class in order to maintain and to improve the artistic instrument—the body. An almost religious nature surrounds this daily ritual, the belief in its principles, and adherence to its practices. This dedication was eloquently acknowledged by the famous Russian ballerina and teacher Olga Preobrazhenskaya (1870–1962) who, when asked why she continued to practice a daily barre long after her performing days were over, replied, "It is my morning prayer."[2]

Advancement from a beginning or elementary ballet class to the intermediate level brings the student closer to this dedicated community. The student becomes more aware of the astounding wealth of ballet's technical vocabulary. Variety of exercises, combinations, and poses seems infinite, as indeed it may be. Soon, too, begins awareness of a thing called style—aspects of interpretation that give different colors or emphases to movements. Before introducing specific technical and stylistic examples of intermediate work, it is important to review a few general concepts commonly encountered in ballet classes beyond the basics.

**STUDIO/
STAGE
DIRECTIONS**

The increased challenges of center floor work include a new appreciation of "the audience," the public "out front." Although perhaps forever unseen by the non-professional ballet student, this critical body of people has "entered" the classroom and must be addressed. That is, students may be told to travel upstage away from the audience, to incline the head toward the public, to stand facing a downstage corner rather than in profile to the audience, etc. The following diagram should be carried mentally to class:

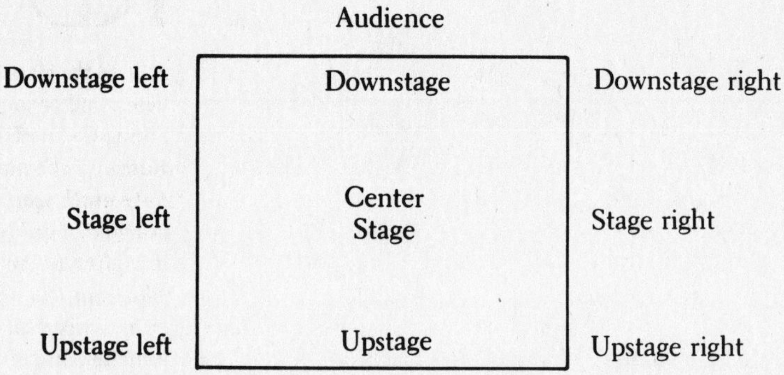

Audience

Downstage left	Downstage	Downstage right
Stage left	Center Stage	Stage right
Upstage left	Upstage	Upstage right

These traditional terms make sense when one realizes that earlier stages were raked or slanted slightly downward toward the audience (most European stages still are). Moving toward the audience was literally moving downward; moving away from the audience was moving upward. When facing directly toward the public (a position sometimes called *de face*), the performer's right side corresponds to the right side of the stage. For simplicity's sake, these directional terms for various points of the studio/stage space will be used hereafter, rather than any numbering system.

**VARIETY OF
INTERPRE-
TATION**

Despite an international language, a legacy from its formative years in French courts and academies, ballet does not have a completely agreed-upon vocabulary or style. This potentially confusing situation usually is shielded from beginners who are introduced to generally accepted basics. But the intermediate student soon is aware of different "systems" that use slightly diverse terminology and stylistic interpretation. Although the French language is never discarded, two of the most important systems are the Italian, or Cecchetti, method and the Russian, or Vaganova, school, named after two famous teachers and the countries where they trained.[3] References to some specific exercises from these masters are found in Chapter 3, including the various *arabesques* used in the two systems.

More importantly, the intermediate student will realize there are many "right" styles, depending upon the situation and preference. Part of the challenge of more advanced ballet levels is to be alert and adaptable to new possibilities and different approaches.

The positions of the arms do not have such universal acceptance as do the five positions of the feet. In an effort to simplify the diverse numbering systems, the following terms will be used for basic arm positions:

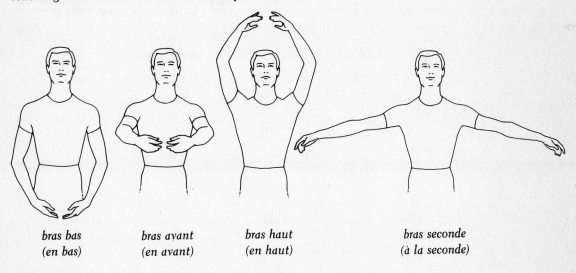

bras bas
(en bas)

bras avant
(en avant)

bras haut
(en haut)

bras seconde
(à la seconde)

To these four basic positions are added three modifications:

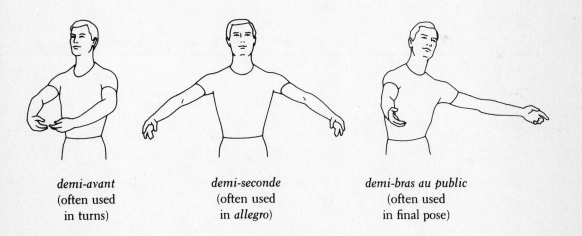

demi-avant
(often used
in turns)

demi-seconde
(often used
in *allegro*)

demi-bras au public
(often used
in final pose)

Other positions are essentially variations of these basic seven (such as one arm *en bas* and the other *demi-seconde*; one arm *en haut* and the other *en avant*, etc.). In general, contemporary styles prefer more extended arms, with hands more centered on the body, than formerly. (See Chapter 5, p. 111, and Chapter 6, p. 135.)

5

DESCRIPTIVE TERMS

Certain descriptive terms are added to the names of movements to indicate the direction taken by the "working foot," that is, the first foot to rise, open, or otherwise leave the original position. These qualifying terms may vary according to different systems, but the following generally accepted order is observed in this book:

Dessus (duh-SUI): the working foot passes in front of the supporting foot.

Dessous (duh-SOO): the working foot passes behind the supporting foot.

Devant (duh-VAHn): the working foot begins from and ends in the front.

Derrière (deh-reeAIR): the working foot begins from and ends in the back.

En avant (ah-na-VAHn): a step is executed forward, typically moving downstage toward the audience.

En arrière (ah-na-reeAIR): a step is executed backward, typically moving upstage away from the audience.

THE FOUR E'S: EQUILIBRIUM, EXTENSION, ELEVATION, ENDURANCE

Equilibrium, or the state of balance, takes on new importance in intermediate classes with the increased emphasis on movements and poses executed on one leg; the security of a strong vertical stance on two feet must now be maintained more often on one foot. As the weight shifts over the center of the supporting foot, it must be lifted well out of the hips so that the horizontal alignment of shoulders over hips, and hip over supporting knee, is maintained. A secure balance over one foot should allow the supporting heel to be raised easily, the body already having anticipated the rise, "because balance is an extension of a movement and not a dead stop."[4]

Frequent poses of balance include the *cou-de-pied* and *retiré* positions. Variations of these poses cited in the following chapters include:

sur le cou-de-pied *sur le cou-de-pied devant* *sur le cou-de-pied derrière*

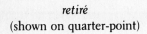

retiré
(shown on quarter-point)

retiré devant
(shown on half-point)

retiré derrière
(shown on three-quarter point)

Extension of the legs takes on greater significance with increased emphasis on balance. Traditionally (since the early nineteenth century), a full extension has meant at the height of the hip. But a distinctive feature of contemporary ballet is a much higher extension for both men and women. So new (since mid-twentieth century) is this common expectation of above-hip-level extension that no term has yet entered the ballet vocabulary to designate such positions. The traditional designations remain:

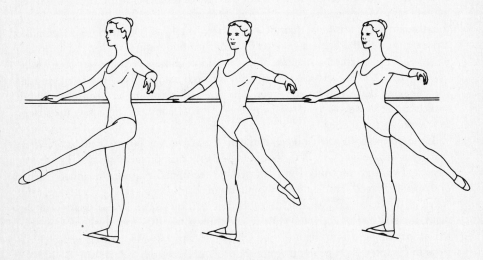

à la demi-hauteur (at half-height, 45 degrees)

à la hauteur (at full height, 90 degrees)

These levels are important for the intermediate student to master. Slow development of both stretch and strength is required for extensions above 90 degrees, because correct body placement cannot be sacrificed for a higher lift of the leg. Adjustments are necessary, however. Some slight sideward tilt of the pelvis occurs even when the leg extends to 90 degrees *à la seconde*. Still, at this level, or with maximum extension, the ribs and shoulders must maintain their horizontal position. In order to facilitate any extension to the back, a simple lifting of the abdominal muscles and an intake of breath help lengthen the spine, thus relieving tightness in the lower back. A lift upward through the waist also is required for high extensions to the front, so that the spine and pelvis can remain erect. This stretching upward between ribs and hip sockets as the leg begins to lift will be referred to as "creating or increasing the space" for movement of the leg.

Elevation in both *petit* and *grand allegro* requires development of an easy *ballon*, that ideal of buoyancy or lively bouncing quality in a dancer's jumps. The larger leaps and springs introduced in intermediate technique require the added quality of suspended flight. This ability to remain momentarily airborne is a result of careful "tuning" of the dance instrument: the body correctly placed in anticipation of the flight, the *port de bras* accurately timed, and the strong push from the floor providing the proper impetus into the air. (See Chapter 5, pp. 110–115, as well as individual steps in Chapter 4.) A push-off from both feet occurs from a *demi-plié*; a push-off from one foot occurs from a *fondu:*

demi-plié in fifth position   two examples of *fondu*

Endurance implies maintaining the energy necessary for the greater technical demands of intermediate ballet. One often-slighted requirement of adequate energy for the dancer is proper nutrition. A basic good sense of correctly balanced nourishment should not be abandoned under pressures to look thinner. The current ballet fad for women with bodies "like toothpick"[5] has caused an alarming rate of excessive thinness, even among nonprofessional students. A serious illness, anorexia nervosa, is not uncommon among young women in ballet who literally starve themselves (sometimes fatally) in an effort to become thinner.

Along with the importance of proper diet there is the necessity of adequate rest. A fatigued or weakened body is accident-prone. Therefore, rather than pushing the body beyond its endurance on a given day, simply watching a class, or taking only the barre work is sometimes advisable. Certainly, any sensation of pain should be recognized as a signal of something wrong. Perhaps it is a warning the body is being strained by improper practice: rolling over on the arches, dropping into the supporting hip, pinching the lower spine, etc. Or it may signal a build-up of tensions from too great an effort: turning out the legs beyond the capacity of the hip sockets, holding a leg in too high an extension, lowering too deeply in a *grand plié*, etc. Moreover, the body may suffer strain without sending out painful signals: tense neck, tightened shoulders, gripped buttocks, and stiff fingers are common manifestations of working too hard, pushing beyond the necessary point. These kinds of tensions consume enormous amounts of energy, depriving the body of the pliability and resilience it needs to meet the technical demands of ballet. Ideally, the dancer tries only "to hold on to the muscles close to the spine, in order to free the rest of the body to be expressive."[6]

At the opposite extreme is relaxing too much during class: allowing the mind to wander while corrections are made or an exercise explained, slumping onto the barre or against the wall while another group performs, even folding the arms and settling into one hip with the weight pushed back onto the knee and heel of the supporting leg. Such behavior and posture causes the body's energy to drop, and extra effort is required to bring it back to proper posture and attention. The dance student cannot afford such loss of energy. Acquiring technique means acquiring discipline.

Properly fitting footwear—tights, or socks, and shoes that do not restrict the natural position of the toes and arches, and that do not cause pressures on the heel or ball of the foot—also contribute importantly to the general maintenance of good body health.

THE "GOOD" CLASS

Most ballet students begin to recognize when they have had (or are having) a "good" class. Such recognition is not always associated with the sense of having performed particularly well. Indeed, many students are unable to define what they intuitively realize: the "good" class has offered them a variety of movement challenges within an overall thematic development seeming to flow from barre to center floor, and results in a feeling of accomplishment and understanding. This is achieved in a variety of ways. For instance, on a given day, several barre exercises may emphasize particular positions of the body, perhaps for a final balance at the end of certain exercises. Later those same positions can be repeated in center floor as part of both *adagio* and *allegro* combinations. The challenge can be to explore those same poses in large, slow movements as well as in small, quick ones. Or, a *port de bras* introduced at barre, as part of a *rond de jambe* series perhaps, can be repeated in center during a *temps lié* exercise and later in a waltz combination.

The teacher's planning strategy often is to work backwards. That is: decide on certain center combinations to be featured in a particular class; next, decide which aspects of those combinations can be extracted for use as center exercises; and finally, decide how to simplify those aspects even further as barre exercises. For instance, if a center combination is to be three quick *changements* followed by an *échappé sauté* to fourth position and a *pirouette en dehors*, an earlier preparation both at barre and in center could be: three *battements dégagés* (alternating closing back, front, back) finishing in *demi-plié* in fifth position, a *dégagé* to the back finishing in fourth position *demi-plié*, and a *relevé devant* (back foot coming to the front of the supporting knee).

Any center combination can benefit from having at least certain of its elements introduced earlier as a barre or center floor exercise. In this way a particular rhythmic pattern can be reinforced; a balanced pose can be reattempted; a theme can be developed for the benefit of mind as well as muscles.

Anatole Vilzak became principal dancer with the Maryinsky Theatre soon after his graduation from the Imperial Ballet Academy in 1915 (see photograph in Chapter 6) and continued his career in the West with Diaghilev's Ballets Russes. Many well-known dancers (including Zoritch) have studied with Vilzak and his late wife, ballerina Ludmilla Schollar. For many years a beloved instructor in professional schools in the United States, Vilzak continues a busy teaching schedule at the San Francisco Ballet School. Photo: Ann Wallace.

Kyra Nichols shown in preparation for pirouettes en dedans. *Photo: Bonnie Kamin.*

Even during August vacations, dancers continue to take daily class. New York City Ballet principal dancers, husband and wife Daniel Duell and Kyra Nichols (center and left), practice in the Berkeley studio directed by Nichols' mother, Sally Streets (in arabesque just behind Duell), a former dancer with NYCB. Photo: Bonnie Kamin.

Formerly a principal dancer with the State Theatre of Münster, Germany, and then with Santa Barbara Ballet Theatre, Tamara Lohrenz now is a member of the Nevada Dance Theatre. She is shown practicing a cabriole in the Santa Barbara studio of the Dance Warehouse. Photo: G. Benton Johnson.

Melissa Hayden, also a student of Vilzak and Schollar, joined the New York City Ballet in 1950 and created principal roles in the Balanchine/Robbins repertory. Following her retirement after twenty-three years with the company, Hayden opened her own ballet school in New York City. A frequent guest teacher, she is shown conducting class at the Los Angeles Ballet School. Photo: Sue Martin.

This is not to belittle the inspired moment, the creative invention "on the spot" that often characterizes classes of fine teachers, but it is to suggest that every instructor should bring a mental outline to class.

Preparatory exercises closely related to certain steps (such as two quick *dégagés à la seconde* done on *demi-pointe* as a preparation for *entrechat quatre*) are important strategies of technical training and familiar aspects of even elementary classes. Students at intermediate levels can begin to analyze steps in order to discover the fundamental movements behind those steps. For instance, the basic design of a *brisé* is a *battement soutenu* closing in fifth position, followed by a *battement dégagé*; for a *ballonné* it is a *battement fondu*; for a *temps de cuisse* it is a *battement dégagé* (or a *petit retiré*, depending upon the style preferred) finishing in a *demi-plié* and followed by a *battement dégagé*. It is essential that these basic components be understood before tackling the step itself. In this way, much frustration can be avoided.

All ballet dancers—both students and professionals—are vulnerable to technical "plateaus," periods when improvement seems perversely elusive. It is easy to point the blame: "I'm too old, my body isn't perfectly proportioned, my turnout isn't a complete 180 degrees." However, many dancers have achieved international acclaim despite all those handicaps. It may be small solace, but it is true nevertheless: "Talent is work."[7] The purpose of this book is to assist in that work, realizing, of course, that the boundaries for intermediate technique are not rigid and a technical syllabus is not universally agreed upon. Moreover, these chapters do not attempt to define or to include all that might be introduced at the intermediate level. It is, after all, the intelligent decision of the instructor that evaluates individual student needs and then establishes the order in which his or her technical vocabulary is expanded. Happily, the work of a ballet student never occurs in isolation; a guide, the ballet instructor, shares the endeavor. But, unhappily, the teacher's efforts and responsibilities often are not fully appreciated. It is well to reflect on this cogent observation directed "To The Pupil" (in 1848) by August Bournonville, one of the nineteenth century's great choreographers and teachers:

> When you have received a good lesson and your teacher praises your industry, remember that his exertion has been greater than yours.[8]

NOTES

1 As told to the author by George Zoritch, for many years *premier danseur* with Ballet Russe de Monte Carlo and Grand Ballet du Marquis de Cuevas. His reference is to the first United States tour, in 1959, by the Bolshoi Ballet and its prima ballerina, Galina Ulanova.

2 As quoted in Elvira Roné, *Olga Preobrazhenskaya* (New York: Marcel Dekker, 1978), p. 124.

3 Enrico Cecchetti (born: Rome, 1850; died: Milan, 1928) studied with Giovanni Lepri, a pupil of Carlo Blasis, and made his adult debut as a dancer at La Scala. He worked in St. Petersburg as dancer and teacher, becoming second ballet master at the Imperial Theatre and creating the roles of Carabosse and

Blue Bird in the Petipa/Tchaikovsky ballet, *Sleeping Beauty*. Later he was engaged by Diaghilev as ballet master for his Ballet Russe company. His many pupils include Pavlova, Nijinsky, Karsavina, de Valois, Lifar, Craske.

Agrippina Vaganova (born: St. Petersburg, 1879; died: Leningrad, 1951) graduated from the St. Petersburg Imperial Ballet Academy in 1897. She was a member of the Maryinsky Ballet, rising to the rank of ballerina by 1915. She retired soon after and joined the Petrograd State Choreographic School, of which she became director in 1934. Some of her famous pupils include Ulanova, Volkova, Semyonova, Dudinskaya.

4 As told to the author by George Zoritch.

5 George Balanchine, as quoted in Selma Jeanne Cohen, *Dance as a Theatre Art* (New York: Dodd, Mead, 1974), p. 157.

6 As told to the author by George Zoritch.

7 Maxim Gorky (the Russian novelist), as quoted in Albert E. Kahn, *Days With Ulanova* (New York: Simon and Schuster, 1962), p. 4. The quote is a particular favorite of Ulanova's.

8 August Bournonville, *My Theatre Life*, trans. Patricia N. McAndrew (Middletown, Conn.: Wesleyan, 1979), p. 63. The period covered is 1848 to 1878.

CHAPTER TWO
BARRE EXERCISES

. . . ballet is a conservative art in the best sense of the term, making daring experiments in the theatre but preserving its traditions in the classroom."

Jack Anderson, 1974.[1]

For all its reliance on tradition, ballet technique always has responded, if somewhat slowly, to changing trends in choreography, costuming, music, and a host of other performance variables. Contemporary ballet choreography, with its increasing emphasis on sleek line, higher extensions, and movements once considered acrobatic, has brought about a gradual change in the ritual of barre work. For one thing, the amount of time spent in barre exercises has increased from thirty minutes or less to sometimes forty-five minutes or more in an average hour-and-a-half class. This is because of the increased strength, control, and suppleness required for contemporary technique. Exercises that develop those attributes tend to be slower than those that prepare for the brilliant foot work of *allegro* characteristic of an older technical style. Poses at barre are held longer, both to build strength and to allow correction of the streamlined design of limbs and body. Thus, the general trend of today's barre work seems to be toward larger exercises, such as *développés*, which involve the entire leg, rather than smaller exercises, such as *petits battements battus*, which work primarily the lower leg.

More than stylistic preferences have nurtured some changes, however. Studies in kinesiology, physical therapy, sports medicine, and anatomy and physiology have caused some dancers to question the appropriateness of *grand plié* as part of the first exercise at barre. The founder of the Dance Kinetic Education Institute in New York City, Raoul Gelabert, declares, "The exercise that taxes the knee most, even when perfectly executed, is the *grand plié*."[2] Perhaps it is time to restructure *plié* exercises, limiting the initial exercise to *demi-pliés*, as was done when the ballet lesson was first codified. (See Chapter 6, p. 128.) Another alternative could be: include slow *battements tendus* and *battements tendus relevés* along with *demi-pliés* and perhaps *relevés* on two feet during the first exercise at barre; in a second or third exercise introduce deeper *pliés* in second position, heels still firmly on the ground; later in the sequence of exercises, incorporate *grand pliés* in first position, being careful to maintain the verticality of the spine and the weight well lifted out of the hips. Later still, add *grand pliés* in fourth and/or fifth positions, always remembering that "Repetition [of *grands pliés*] should be done with moderation, using good judgment to pace the momentum and dynamic quality of the movement."[3]

Other changes in the traditional class format are occurring even before barre work and, while taking many forms, represent further responses to the new dimensions of technique and the awareness of dancers' physiques. Pre-barre warm-ups—either lying or sitting on the floor, standing or moving in center floor, or at the barre itself—have come out of the hallways and dressing rooms and into the formal sequence of the lesson. Not all classes, of course, can allow time for incorporation of pre-barre exercises, and dancers will continue to practice favorite exercises on their own before class. For those wanting some more exercises, consider the following gentle warm-up sequence for slow practice before *pliés*.

**WARM-UP
SEQUENCE
BEFORE *PLIÉS***

1. Face the barre, legs parallel, feet about three inches apart, and hands resting lightly on the barre. Raise the right heel as high as possible while keeping the ball of the foot firmly on the ground. Lower the right heel and at the same time raise the left heel. Continue "treading" in this manner eight times, carefully raising and lowering the heel in line with the center of the foot each time.

Do not press back on the knees; keep the weight well lifted upward and over the balls of the feet.

2. Keeping the legs parallel, fully arch the foot each time the heel is lifted, pointing the toes strongly downward toward the ground. Roll down through the foot in a toe-ball-heel manner each time. Do this four times, alternating legs. Continue four times more while gradually moving backward away from the barre until the arms are fully extended.

3. Press both heels firmly to the floor, legs straight, back and neck lengthened. There should be a sense of a direct, straight line from the top of the head to the heels. Continue this stretch, without bouncing, for eight slow counts.

4. Then, without releasing the barre, take the hips backward by bending forward from the hip sockets until the torso is parallel to the floor. Continue to keep the sense of length in the spine through the top of the head. Do not allow the rib cage to fall forward, tending to sway the spine. Keep the legs straight if possible, but never pushed backward, and the weight forward over the balls of the feet. (Those with tightly knit bodies may prefer to release the knees slightly in this position, thus preventing muscle strain.) Continue to stretch in this position, without bouncing, for eight counts. Repeat exercises 3 and 4.

5. Then, releasing the barre, *demi-plié*, legs still parallel, and allow the torso to round over the legs. Sense the curve of the entire spine, from coccyx to the cervical vertebrae. Allow the neck, shoulders, and arms to relax as the hands rest on the floor. Slowly straighten the knees as much as possible without strain, keeping the weight forward over the balls of the feet, and uncurl the spine, vertebra by vertebra, to a standing position, taking eight slow counts for this entire sequence. Then, step forward toward the barre, stand parallel to it, place the left hand on it.

6. Raise the right arm overhead. Without bending the elbow, reach the arm backward and high, letting it pulse or reach gently backward four times. Sense

the stretching of the shoulder area and the opening of the chest. Continue to open the arm farther backward until it reaches shoulder level, turning the head to look into the right hand. Keep the hips to the front so that the twist comes from the waist and neck only. Take four slow counts to arrive at this position.

7. Lower the working arm, curve the spine, *demi-plié* (legs are still parallel), and bend slightly forward from the waist. Swing the working arm backward and overhead, straightening the knees and spine to an upright position. Slowly lower the arm in front of the body.

8. Raise the right knee, pulling it close to the body either with the right hand placed just below the knee or the lower arm behind and under the knee. Hold this position four slow counts. Gradually open the right knee to the side and turn out the supporting leg, allowing the weight of the right leg to be supported by the right arm so that the thigh rests easily in its joint. Keep the shoulders and hips in alignment without any twisting to the right. Hold this position for four slow counts. Release and lower the leg. Repeat exercises 6, 7, and 8 on the other side.

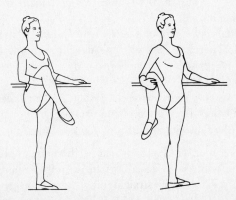

Barre exercises, no matter how simple or complex, need a clear, clean beginning and ending. This requires that time be given to standing quietly ready before making an appropriate preparation with the arms and head. The musical preparation, perhaps four measures rather than merely two chords, should allow time for a deliberate movement preparation. The following is one example:

Raise both arms from *bas* to *avant*. Open the arm nearest the barre, slightly turning the head toward the hand as it lightly takes the railing (fingers resting on top of the barre, thumb along the side of the barre rather than below it). Raise the other arm *en haut*, slightly lifting and turning the head to look in the direction of, but not directly at, the raised hand. (Depending upon the exercise to follow and stylistic preferences, the head may remain straight, rather than tilted either slightly away from or toward the outside arm.)

Exercises at the intermediate level frequently finish with sustained balances. Again, time must be allowed for the pose to be held and a proper completion made. For instance, if the balance is on *demi-pointe* in the *retiré* position, arms *en haut*, the finish might be the following:

After holding the pose, lower the raised foot to fifth position *en demi-pointes*. Without moving the arms, open the back foot very slightly in order to lower the heels in fifth position *demi-plié*. Straighten the knees while opening the arms to the side. Inhale as this last movement is made, turning the head slightly away from the barre. Exhale as both arms lower *en bas*. Hold this final pose.

ADDITIONAL BARRE EXERCISES

The following list of barre exercises builds upon those already incorporated in most basic ballet training. Although others might have been included, these exercises are ones commonly found in classes that have progressed beyond the basics.

MORE BATTEMENTS

BATTEMENT SOUTENU (baht-MAHn soo-teh-NIU)

Definition Literally, a sustained beating, this *battement* involves a *fondu* or bend on the supporting leg.

Purpose The initial movement of a *battement soutenu* is also the initial movement of many steps. Therefore, the exercise develops coordination and control necessary for executing *glissades*, *assemblés*, *pas de bourrées*, *pas de basques*, and *soutenus* turns, to name a few.

Description *Battements soutenus* can be done to any direction, and are frequently practiced *en croix*. Two forms of the exercise are equally valid, but they should be learned in the following order:

1. Slide the working foot, knee straight, along the floor to *pointe tendue* while bending the supporting knee. (See Chapter 1, p. 9, drawing at right.) Return the foot to fifth position while straightening the supporting knee.

2. Make a *petit développé* to *pointe tendue* while bending the supporting knee. The return to fifth position may be made to *demi-pointes* as the supporting knee straightens. The exercise then begins again from the fifth position *demi-pointes*.

Cautions   Do not change the alignment of the pelvis or "sit" into the supporting hip as the knee bends. When taking *battements soutenus* to the back, be especially aware of extending the space from lower ribs to upper thighs in order for the leg to open easily.

Suggestions   Proper placement of the hips can be practiced by first taking a *demi-plié* in fifth position before sliding or developing the working foot to *pointe tendue*. This exercise, as well as the *battements soutenus* described above, also may be practiced with the working leg extended to 45 degrees.

BATTEMENT TENDU RELEVÉ (baht-mahn tahn-diu ruh-leh-VAY)

Definition   A beating or *battement* stretched and relifted, in which the heel lowers in the open position, then relifts *(relevés)* before closing. There is no rise to *demi-pointe*.

Purpose   This exercise is an efficient way to achieve a variety of benefits: strength and development of the insteps, increased sense of space between the lower ribs and upper thighs, and smooth transfer of weight from one foot to both feet.

Description   *Battement tendu relevé* is learned *à la seconde*, but later may be taken *en croix*. Slide the working foot out to *pointe tendue*, keeping the weight held over the straight supporting leg. Release the instep, lower the heel, and transfer the weight equally to both feet. Then relift the heel, re-arch the foot, and return the weight over the supporting leg. Slide the working foot into fifth position.

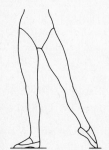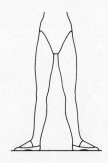

BATTEMENT TENDU RELEVÉ

Cautions   Hips and shoulders must be kept in alignment when the weight shifts from one foot to both feet, a particular challenge when the exercise is taken *en croix*. Keep the toes of the working foot in contact with the floor during the lowering and relifting of the heel.

Suggestions Inhaling when the heel lowers to the open position seems to help extend the space between lower ribs and upper thighs, and thus allows a full extension of the legs. Begin the exercise to the side along a path indicated by the degree of turnout. Thus, when the heel is lowered, it may be slightly forward of second position if the degree of turnout so indicates.

BATTEMENT DÉGAGÉ PIQUÉ (baht-mahn day-gah-zhay pee-KAY)

Definition A beating or *battement* disengaged from the floor, then lowered to *pointe tendue* with a sharp pricking action, and quickly raised again. *Piqué* in this instance does not indicate a step onto *demi-pointe*, but rather the sharp, pricked movement.

Purpose Usually performed quickly, these *dégagés* build lightness and speed in the legs, particularly valuable for later work *en pointe*.

Description Brush the working foot slightly off the floor, then quickly lower to *pointe tendue*. From there, continue to rapidly raise and lower the foot the desired number of times, keeping the foot fully arched until it slides to fifth position at the end of the sequence.

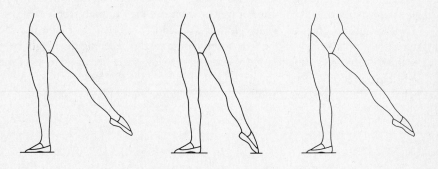

BATTEMENT DÉGAGÉ PIQUÉ

Cautions Both legs should be fully extended throughout the exercise. The toes of the working foot must touch the floor very lightly before rebounding into the air. There is no relaxation of the arched foot until it slides into fifth position.

Suggestions The accent of the exercise usually is on the light but sharp tap of the toes on the floor: brush the foot off the floor (count *and*), lower the toes to *pointe tendue* (count *one*), relift the leg (count *and*), continue lowering and lifting the foot the desired number of times, and close to fifth position on the last beat of the sequence.

Definition Beatings or *battements* that swing forward and backward like the clapper on a bell *(cloche)*.

Purpose When done *par terre*, the exercise introduces the smooth, rapid passing of the whole foot through first position necessary for more complicated exercises, such as *ronds de jambe à terre*. When performed with a brush of the leg into the air, the *battements* are a useful limbering exercise. They are learned prior to *battements en balançoire* (see below).

Description From first position, slide the working foot forward to *pointe tendue*, return it to first position, and immediately slide it backward to *pointe tendue*. Because the *battements* usually occur in a series, they are done with a continuous swing of the leg forward and backward through the first position. They may be done higher, as *battements dégagés en cloche*, and later as *grands battements en cloche*.

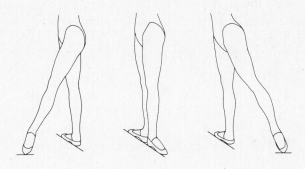

BATTEMENTS EN CLOCHE

Cautions The working foot must pass carefully through first position before and after each *battement* so that there is no rolling of the arch or loss of turnout. The supporting leg must remain motionless in a strong vertical line. The torso does not tilt forward or backward, as it does in *battements en balançoire*, which are taken with a higher swing of the leg.

Suggestions The exercise can be learned with a pause both at *pointe tendue* and in first position, but soon the *battements* should be practiced as a continuous swing, with gradually increasing speed. Once they are learned *par terre*, they may be practiced with gradually increasing height. To avoid dangerous arching at the waistline during the backward swing, keep the weight well forward over the supporting leg, and "create the space" by a strong lift of the abdominal muscles as the torso leans slightly forward.

BATTEMENT DÉVELOPPÉ (baht-mahn day-vloh-PAY)

Definition   A beating or *battement* developed through the *retiré* position before being extended to a point in the air.

Purpose   The developed *battement* is part of many movements in more advanced *allegro* steps, such as *ballotté*. As an exercise, it builds control and strength in the abdomen, back, and legs.

Description   The exercise begins from a closed position, first or fifth. Draw the working foot quickly to the ankle, then without pause bring it to the *retiré* position before briskly extending the leg to the desired position (front, side, or back) in the air. The leg remains straight as it is lowered and the foot returned to the closed position. The reverse of this exercise (*battement, retiré,* close) sometimes is called *enveloppé.*

BATTEMENT DÉVELOPPÉ

Cautions   To attain the required cleanness of the *battement*, the foot must clearly touch the supporting knee before the leg extends. The thigh of the working leg must remain carefully turned out throughout the exercise, and the supporting leg must remain steady.

Suggestions   Learn the exercise to the side before attempting it *en croix.* "Break down" the exercise, that is, give a count for each movement: from the first position, *retiré* (count *one*), extend to second position at 45 degrees or 90 degrees (count *two*), lower to *pointe tendue* (count *three*), and close to first position (count *four*). Later, the entire sequence is taken from fifth position in only two counts: *retiré* (count *and*), extend (count *one*), and close (count *two*).

BATTEMENT FRAPPÉ DOUBLE (baht-mahn fray-pay DOO-bluh)

Definition   Literally, a double beating or *battement* struck.

Purpose   Increased speed and precision for petit *allegro* are attributes of this exercise.

Description From *pointe tendue à la seconde*, bring the foot inward and beat it in front of and immediately behind the supporting ankle, then brush the foot to the side as in a *battement frappé*. The action is then reversed: beat the foot in back of the supporting ankle and immediately pass it in front before brushing outward. (The toes and ball of the working foot typically do not brush the floor on the way inward.)

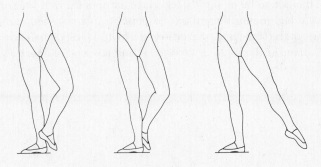

BATTEMENT FRAPPÉ DOUBLE

Cautions The beat occurs from the lower leg only; therefore, when performed to the side, the thigh must remain stationary as the knee bends, allowing the foot to beat quickly against the supporting ankle. When the exercise is performed with the *frappé* brushing forward or backward, the thigh must remain well turned out even as it moves in the direction indicated by the *battement frappé*. The flexing of the ankle (see below) during the beat should not result in a flexing of the toes also.

Suggestions *Battements frappés doubles* usually follow a series of single *frappés*. They first should be practiced slowly *à la seconde*: beat in front (count *one*), pass in back (count *two*), brush *à la seconde* (count *three*), and hold the extended position (count *four*). Reverse the action. Later, as speed increases, the entire beating action occurs on count "*and*" before the brush of the *battement frappé*. The exercise later may be performed with the supporting foot on *demi-pointe*. The position of the working foot at the supporting ankle varies according to different stylistic preferences, the pointed foot being either slightly released with the toes reaching toward the ground, or entirely released and strongly flexed with the sole of the foot parallel to the floor. In either case, the foot remains aligned with the corresponding knee, thus not allowed to twist (sickle) inward or outward.

ROND DE JAMBE EN L'AIR (rohn duh zhahnb ahn LAIR)

Definition A round or circular movement of the leg in the air, the action being from below the knee.

MORE *RONDS DE JAMBE*

Purpose The thigh becomes firm and strong as the lower portion of the leg gains in speed and articulation. The brilliant action of this exercise is found in the advanced *allegro* step *rond de jambe en l'air sauté*.

Description The exercise begins with the working leg in second position at 45 degrees or slightly higher. To perform the *rond de jambe en dehors*, bend the knee of the working leg, allowing the foot to travel in an outward oval-shaped pattern without disturbing the position of the thigh: the foot moves slightly backward, then to the top of the calf of the supporting leg, and continues the oval pattern by moving slightly forward before returning to second position *à la demi-hauteur*. The action may continue, or the straight leg can be lowered to fifth position behind. To perform *en dedans*, *battement* the leg again to the side and reverse the direction of the oval pattern.

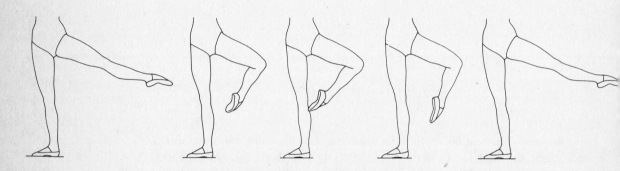

ROND DE JAMBE EN L'AIR

Cautions Once the second position *à la demi-hauteur* is established, the thigh of the working leg must remain immobile throughout the circling action of the foot. Both legs remain well turned out, the body balanced over the supporting foot. Each *rond de jambe* is completed by a careful straightening, not snapping, of the working knee. Do not "beat" the toes in front or in back of the supporting leg; instead, smoothly touch the calf lightly with the toes before passing forward or backward.

Suggestions Although this exercise can be performed at 90 degrees (*à la hauteur*), the toes thus passing the knee of the supporting leg rather than its calf, it is best begun at a lower level. In order to ensure that the action is from the knee down without movement of the thigh, the following preliminary exercise is helpful: brush the working leg to second position at 45 degrees (count *one*), bend the working knee and, *without* circling the foot, merely bring the toes directly in to touch the calf of the supporting leg (count *two*), extend the leg again to second position, fully straightening the knee (count *three*), and lower the straight leg to fifth position behind (count *four*). Repeat the exercise, closing front. Later the circling motion occurs on count "*and*," while the extension to second position occurs on the beat.

Definition A large round of the leg on the ground, in actuality a semicircle of the foot on the ground while the supporting leg is bent *(en fondu)*. The toes of the working foot are extended farther from the body, thus the arc outlined is large *(grand)* compared with a regular *rond de jambe à terre*.

Purpose The exercise, often combined with arm and head movement, improves coordination and imparts a valuable dance quality even at the barre. *Pas de basque glissé* incorporates some movements from this exercise.

Description To perform *en dehors*, *demi-plié* in first or fifth position, extend the working leg to *pointe tendue* to the front. Keep the supporting knee bent as the working foot describes a semicircle on the ground, passing through second position to *pointe tendue* to the back. The action can continue through first position *demi-plié*, or the foot can close to first or fifth position behind as the supporting knee straightens. To perform *en dedans*, reverse the direction of the semicircle.

en dehors

en dedans

GRAND ROND DE JAMBE À TERRE

Cautions Keep the abdominal muscles well lifted, especially when the leg reaches *pointe tendue* to the back. The working foot must remain fully arched, heel well lifted but toes remaining on the floor, throughout the circular movement. The supporting knee *en fondu* must remain well turned out, in line with the supporting foot.

Suggestions Exercises preliminary to this one include *battements soutenus en croix* and *demi-grand rond de jambe à terre*. In the latter, the working foot makes a quarter-circle to second position as the supporting knee bends, then closes in first or fifth position as the supporting knee straightens.

For arm and head coordination during *rond de jambe en dehors*, the following *port de bras* can be used: lower the outside arm *en bas* as the *fondu* begins, raise the arm *en avant* and incline the head slightly away from the barre as the leg extends to the front, open the arm *à la seconde* and straighten the head as the leg moves to the side, leave the arm in second position but incline the head slightly toward the barre as the leg goes to the back. For *rond de jambe en dedans*, the arm movement is the same, but the head inclines first toward the barre and finishes away from the barre. In this manner, the head is always inclined in the direction of the leg that is in front, whether it be the working or the supporting leg.

ROND DE JAMBE EN ATTITUDE (rohn duh zhahnb ahn ah-tee-TEWD)
Definition A round (semicircle) of the leg in an *attitude*.

Purpose In addition to establishing correct *attitude* positions, this exercise is helpful in improving turnout, control, and placement later required in *grands ronds de jambe en l'air*.

Description To perform *en dehors*, brush the working foot forward, raising the leg to a low *attitude devant*, the knee well bent. Maintaining that same angle, move the thigh to the side, then continue circling it to the back. Then, straighten the

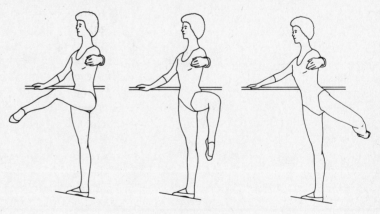

ROND DE JAMBE EN ATTITUDE

knee, extending the leg to a low *arabesque*. The action can continue by brushing through first position, or the exercise can finish by lowering the leg to fifth position behind. To perform *en dedans*, reverse the direction of the pattern.

Cautions   The thigh of the working leg should be in line with the corresponding shoulder in *attitude devant* and *derrière*. When the thigh is carried to the side, keep the foot in a direct line under the knee if the exercise is performed with a low *attitude*, as described above. In *attitude derrière*, the pelvis will tilt slightly forward, then straighten to the upright position when the leg moves to the side or lowers to the closed position.

Suggestions   Allow a full measure of a waltz rhythm for each portion of the exercise. Later the entire circling of the thigh can be done in two measures. The exercise can be performed with the knee higher and only half-bent, but this is practiced after the lower positions are learned. The head can incline toward the forward leg, as in the previous exercise.

GRAND ROND DE JAMBE EN L'AIR (grahn rohn duh zhahnb ahn LAIR)

Definition   A large round (semicircle) of the leg in the air.

Purpose   Control and balance for *adagio* movement are gained from this exercise, emphasizing, as it does, the important pelvic adjustments necessary for the leg to travel in the air from front to side to back, and vice versa.

Description   The action may begin either with a *développé* or a straight extension of the working leg. To perform *en dehors*, develop or extend the working leg to 45 degrees or 90 degrees *devant*, then move the leg to second position, maintaining the same level in the air, and continue circling at that level to the back. (See Chapter 1, pp. 7–8, for drawings of positions in *grand rond de jambe*.) The exercise can continue by brushing through first position or by passing to the front through the *retiré* position. To perform *en dedans*, reverse the direction of the pattern.

Cautions   The supporting leg must remain strongly extended and turned out throughout the exercise. The shoulders must not twist toward the moving leg. As the leg moves from the side to the back, the pelvis tilts slightly forward to allow the leg to maintain its level in the air. The pelvis must return to its normal upright position as the leg moves from the back to the side or to the front.

Suggestions   An important preliminary exercise is *demi-grand rond de jambe en l'air*: develop or extend the leg to the front or back, circle it only to the side and lower to first or fifth position. Coordination of breath and *port de bras* are helpful in both the *demi-grand* and *grand rond de jambe*: raise the outside arm *en avant* as the leg extends to the front or back, inhale and raise the arm *en haut* as the leg moves to the side. The intake of breath and lift of arm increase the upward stretch of the body, allowing the leg greater freedom for the circular motion. When the leg moves from the side to the back, the arm can open to second position or, preferably, extend forward to *arabesque*, a position that helps keep the shoulders level and the body and working leg equally balanced over the supporting leg.

PAS DE CHEVAL (pah duh shuh-VAHL)

Definition   Literally, step of the horse, a small, quick *développé* to *pointe tendue* (or a few inches above the ground). The term *pas de cheval* usually applies to an *allegro* step performed *devant* (see Chapter 4, p. 80), but it also can refer to this exercise.

Purpose   Speed and precision in arching and extending the foot, sometimes combined with a *fondu*, help prepare for brisk *allegro* movements.

Description   From *pointe tendue à la seconde*, slide the working foot to fifth position front, knees straight, and immediately arch the foot in front of the supporting ankle. Straighten the working knee as the foot extends to the side, either to *pointe tendue* or slightly above the ground. The action is repeated from fifth position back.

Cautions   The foot should relax momentarily in the fifth position before arching strongly, heel well pressed forward. The toes remain fully pointed as the leg develops to the open position.

Suggestions   After the exercise is learned to the side, it should be practiced slowly *en croix*: close to fifth position (count *one*), arch the foot (count *two*), *développé* to the front (counts *three* and *four*), repeat the exercise to the side, then to the back, and again to the side. Later, it is effectively done in a quick waltz rhythm: close to fifth position and immediately arch the foot (count *one*), *développé* (counts *two* and *three*). The arching of the foot and the *développé* may occur with the supporting leg in *fondu*, and the close to fifth position may be to *demi-pointes*. Thus, when performed to the front, the exercise incorporates the movements of the *allegro* step, *pas de cheval*.

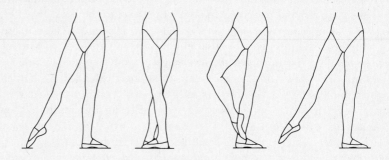

PAS DE CHEVAL

DÉVELOPPÉ EN FONDU (day-vlo-pay ahn fohn-DIU)

Definition   A developing movement of one leg as the supporting leg bends.

Purpose   By simultaneously bending one leg while developing the other, the dancer works for coordination and control necessary for *adagio* and grand *allegro* movements that use these same motions.

Description Draw the working foot up to the supporting knee (this *retiré* position can be with the pointed toe in front of, at the side of, or behind the supporting knee depending upon the direction of the following *développé*), then unfold the leg to the open position as the supporting leg lowers in *fondu*. Return the extended foot either to fifth position or to the *retiré* position as the supporting leg straightens.

Cautions A higher *développé* is possible when the supporting knee is allowed to bend, as in this exercise. Therefore, special care need be taken to keep the pelvis in its upright position when the leg develops to the front or side. However, when the leg develops to the back, the pelvis may tilt forward, but, in so doing, the abdominal muscles must be especially well lifted.

Suggestions When performing this exercise in a moderate tempo, coordination of breath and *port de bras* may occur as follows: as the foot comes to the *retiré* position, raise the outside arm *en avant* and begin to inhale; as the leg develops, open the arm to second position and continue breathing in; as the leg closes, exhale and lower the arm *en bas*.

DÉVELOPPÉ EN FONDU

DÉVELOPPÉ PASSÉ (day-vloh-pay pah-SAY)

Definition A developed movement passing from front to back or back to front through the *retiré* position.

Purpose Control of the spine and lightness of the leg are two attributes of *développé passé*.

Description To perform *en arrière*, lift the working leg, fully extended, to 45 degrees or 90 degrees *devant*. Keeping the thigh well turned out, bring the foot in to the *retiré* position. Then, develop the leg to 45 degrees or 90 degrees *derrière*. To perform *en avant*, reverse the direction of the action.

Cautions The exercise should be attempted only after the tilting and straightening of the pelvis is well understood, because the abdominal muscles must be well lifted and the shoulders free of tension during the extensions to the back. The turnout of both legs must be carefully maintained as the foot passes the knee and develops to the new direction.

Suggestions Learn the exercise by allowing a full count or measure for each movement: brush the leg into the air (count *one*), *retiré* (count *two*), begin the *développé* through the *attitude* position (count *three*), fully extend the leg (count *four*). To repeat the exercise to the same direction, brush the straight leg directly through first position and continue as above. Later, the exercise is taken quickly in two counts: brush the leg into the air (count *one*), *retiré* (count *and*), *développé* (count *two*). To help maintain turnout in the developing leg, lead forward with the heel from the *retiré* position, but lead backward with the knee, making sure that the knee is well behind the corresponding shoulder.

DÉVELOPPÉ PASSÉ

DÉVELOPPÉ-ROTATION (day-vlo-pay-roh-tah-SYON)

Definition A developed movement followed by a quarter- or half-rotation on the supporting leg, a movement related to *demi-fouetté* and *fouetté en relevé* (see Chapter 3, pp. 61–62).

Purpose More than most exercises, this one challenges the strength and control of the supporting leg, which rotates and thus turns the entire pelvis to the new direction.

Description To perform with a half-turn to *arabesque*, *développé* the outside leg to the front. Bend the supporting leg (*fondu*), then rise to *demi-pointe* (*relevé*) and make a quarter-turn to face the barre. The forward leg now has rotated in the hip socket and the position is *à la seconde*. The movement can continue with a quarter-turn to *arabesque en demi-pointe*, or another *fondu* and *relevé* may accompany the turn. The complete half-turn then finishes in *arabesque fondu*. To perform with a half-turn to *quatrième devant*, reverse the direction of the action: develop the inside leg to the back, turn to the barre and continue turning to *quatrième devant*.

Cautions   The shoulders must remain level and squarely facing each new direction. The extended leg must be well stretched away from the body in order to facilitate the rotation in both hips.

Suggestions   First practice the *en dehors* exercise *à terre*: extend the outside leg to the front by making a *petit développé* to *pointe tendue* and bend the supporting leg, rise to quarter-point and turn to face the barre allowing the extended leg to move slightly forward in order to maintain correct line of turnout. Lower the heel of the supporting leg and *fondu*. Rise again to quarter-point and turn to *arabesque*. Again lower the heel and *fondu*. Reverse the direction of the action for practicing the exercise *en dedans*. Later, the leg is developed to 45 degrees or 90 degrees and maintained at that level during the entire rotation. Allow the muscles on the insides of the legs to relax slightly during the *fondus* so that they may stretch strongly during the *relevés* and rotations. Inhale during each rise and turn, exhale during each *fondu*.

DÉVELOPPÉ-ROTATION

All of the following exercises, which are a form of stretching, should be performed smoothly without pauses so that the movement is fluid and muscle tension is prevented.

MORE *CORPS ET BRAS EXERCISES* (kor ay brah eg-zehr-SEES)

CAMBRÉ CIRCLING THE BODY (kahn-BRAY)
Definition   A bending and circling of the body from the waist.

Purpose   The curving and circling motion of the upper body while the pelvis and legs remain stationary improves flexibility as well as control of the spine. Similar movements are found in advanced steps involving *renversé* (rahn-vehr-SAY).

Description   Raise the outside arm from second position to overhead, and bend the body from the waist sideward toward the barre. With the arm remaining overhead, curve the upper body diagonally forward toward the barre, then continue to circle directly forward and sideward away from the barre. The circle continues as the upper body curves backward, the arm remaining overhead, and is completed with a return to the sideward bend to the barre before coming to the upright position. The direction can be reversed: bend the body away from the barre, then circle forward and sideward toward the barre, continue the circle to the back and sideward away from the barre.

Cautions   The pelvis should remain level, the turnout firmly controlled, as the body circles from the waist. The head must not drop in the direction of the bend, but instead remain in the same relationship to the shoulders and spine as when the exercise began. Try not to tense the muscles under the shoulder blades or at the back of the neck.

Suggestions   The exercise may be performed in first or fifth positions. Inhale as the sideward bend begins in order to create the space for the elongated curve. Exhale during the circling motion to the front and side. As the critical curve from side to back begins, inhale again and lengthen the neck from the spine. Imagine that the head directs the circling motion, even though it does not move out of alignment. Lift the abdominal muscles inward and upward for the entire circular pattern. Later, the exercise can be performed with a deeper bend forward from the hip sockets, a movement used in *grands port de bras* in center exercises.

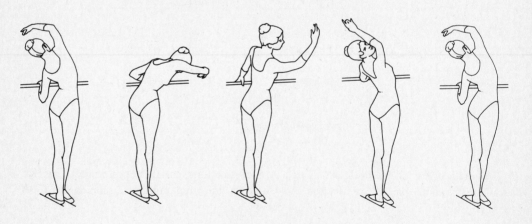

CAMBRÉ CIRCLING THE BODY

PORT DE BRAS EN FONDU (por duh brah ahn foh*n*-DIU)
Definition   Carriage of the arms with a forward bend of the body while the supporting leg is bent.

Purpose   This exercise stretches the body while it develops a flow of movement in the upper body and arms, along with a strong balance over one leg.

Description   To perform *à la quatrième devant*, extend the outside leg forward to *pointe tendue* while bending the supporting leg, as in a *battement soutenu*. Keeping the spine straight and the outside arm *à la seconde*, incline the torso forward from the hip sockets. Bend the torso lower, allowing the spine to curve and the arm to round overhead. Return the body to the upright position while straightening the supporting leg. To perform with the leg *à la quatrième derrière*, extend either leg backward to *pointe tendue* while bending the other leg in *fondu*. The extended foot may remain pointed or the heel may lower to the ground. The bending action continues as above. (Both forward stretches also can be done with the back remaining straight and the head kept in line with the spine.)

PORT DE BRAS EN FONDU

Cautions   All versions of this exercise are particularly challenging to the supporting leg: the supporting foot must be firmly anchored, thigh well turned out, and the body weight evenly balanced between the big and little toe joints and the heel. The extended leg must not bear weight, nor should weight settle down into the supporting hip. Although the chin can lift when the exercise begins, that action should result from an intake of breath and slight lift of the chest and should not cause strain in the neck. A bend backward *(cambré)* can be taken in these *fondu* positions, but, at this level of training, they are best done with a straight supporting leg. Therefore, only the forward bend is described here.

Suggestions   To keep the body from settling into the supporting hip, inhale as the forward bend begins, lift the abdominal muscles, and continue that lift as the spine curves forward. To help prevent tension in the shoulder area, keep the arm rounded, allow the head to bend slightly forward when the spine curves forward, and then let it initiate or "lead" the body to the upright position without any shortening of the back of the neck. The extended leg will draw closer to the body as the supporting knee straightens.

PORT DE BRAS AND *CAMBRÉ EN DEMI-POINTES*
(kah*n*-BRAY ahn d'mee PWaH*n*T)

Definition   Carriage of the arms with a forward, backward, sideward, or circular bend of the torso with the body balanced on half-toe.

Purpose   Increased stretch of the legs, greater control over the turnout at the hip sockets, and more flexibility and strength in the spine are some of the goals of *port de bras* and *cambré* when taken on the *demi-pointes*. This position strengthens the feet as well.

Description   After a rise to *demi-pointes* (in any position of the feet, but most frequently fifth position), the bend of the torso in any direction should conform to the general rules of *port de bras* and *cambré* when taken with the soles of the feet on the ground: the forward bend can be made from above the waist, from the waist, or from the hip sockets; the sideward bend curves the spine from the waist or above it; the backward bend arches the spine from above the waist. (In later phases of training, the backward bend can be deeper, thus arching more from the waist.)

PORT DE BRAS AND CAMBRÉ EN DEMI-POINTES

Cautions The straight vertical line of the legs should not alter as the body bends or circles in any direction. Care should be taken, especially for those with hyper-extended knees, never to lock the knees or press them backward during the exercise. The balance on the balls of the feet is firmly placed over the center of each foot, ideally with the weight of the body distributed evenly over all ten toes. (Varying foot shapes may require some adjustment in this position. For instance, feet with sharply tapered toes may need to shift the balance more toward the first three toes.)

Suggestions Stretches like these are practiced only after their movements are well understood when performed with the soles of the feet on the ground. As in all deep *port de bras* and *cambrés*, the movements should be done smoothly without pause. A lift of the abdominal muscles is important for maintaining the proper alignment of the pelvis and for raising the weight out of the hips.

STRETCHES ON THE BARRE

Leg-on-the-barre stretches frequently conclude barre work at the intermediate level. Some classes offer such a stretching sequence just prior to the final *grands battements* series, others utilize the final *battements* as a preliminary limbering exercise for the stretches themselves. Still other classes offer stretches sitting or lying on the floor, or as an after-class activity. In all instances, the body should be thoroughly warmed up before any such stretches begin.

If barre stretches are attempted, they require the proper height of barre in order for the movements to be safely and effectively performed. Ideally, a studio is equipped with barres of different heights. Sometimes, when lower levels are needed, a straight chair-back or stool can be used. What is required is a rail whose height will allow both legs to remain straight and the pelvis upright, not tipped, when one leg is placed on the barre to the front or to the side. Stretches with the leg in *arabesque* on the barre should be attempted *only* if the dancer has sufficient control and flexibility, particularly in the spine, to allow the stretch to occur without tension, distortion of alignment, or any discomfort. Suppleness, not pain, should be the product of careful stretches. Individual hip structure also must help determine when, if, and how stretches on the barre will be beneficial. Assuming the student is ready, and the proper rail height is available, the following sequence is offered as one example of a stretch on the barre:

1. Stand in fifth position facing the barre, holding it with both hands. *Grand plié,* straighten the legs, *soussus,* and raise the front foot *sur le cou-de-pied* as the back heel lowers.
2. *Retiré* slowly, keeping the hips and shoulders parallel with the barre. Raise the thigh to the side as high as possible, allowing the angle at the knee to open up slightly. Pause in this *attitude* position *à la seconde* in order to release the contraction of the muscles in the lower spine and in back of the knee, thus allowing them greater freedom to lift and extend the leg.

3. Continue the *développé* of the leg to second position and carefully place the foot on the barre. (Often a dancer is advised to place the heel on the barre rather than the back of the ankle. Alternatively, a towel or pad under the ankle may be required. The important consideration is to minimize any pressure on the Achilles tendon as the weight of the leg rests on the barre.)

4. Now, *fondu* on the supporting leg, carefully bending the knee over the center of the foot. Straighten the leg and rise to *demi-pointe*, balancing the weight over the ball of the foot. Lower the heel, lifting the abdominal muscles and centering the weight over the foot.

5. Continue by opening the arm opposite the raised leg to second position. Bring the arm overhead. Inhale, increasing the sense of length in the spine, and bend slightly sideward from the waist. Exhale, gradually bending lower from this diagonal reach into a deeper sideward curve over the leg. Keep the arm

STRETCHES ON THE BARRE

rounded overhead, neck lengthened, and shoulders free of tension. The focus may be forward or toward the leg on the barre. Pause in this position.

6. Return along the same path to the upright position, arm still rounded overhead. Turn the face toward the inside of the raised elbow. Inhale, increasing the sense of space between the ribs and pelvis, lift the chest upward, and bend slightly backward. Without disturbing the upright position of the pelvis, gradually increase the backward bend from above the waist only. Keep the arm rounded overhead and in line with, not behind, the shoulder. The head remains slightly turned toward the raised arm, the neck long but not tense, the abdominal muscles well lifted, and the supporting leg firmly straight.

7. Begin to exhale, and return along the same path to the upright position, centering the arm in front of the body. The stretch may be repeated, or the leg on the barre lifted and carefully lowered to fifth position.

The same stretch can be performed sideward away from the leg on the barre, or forward over the leg. In the latter case, the dancer faces the barre on a very shallow diagonal so that the inside hip is quite close to the railing. Usually the inside hand rests on the barre and the raised arm corresponds to the raised leg. Whatever the position in which stretches are done, it should offer a pleasing design to the beholder. Whatever the goal of the stretch, it should be pursued through moderate, slow means, never through harsh or rapid action.

PUTTING IT ALL TOGETHER

Early-nineteenth-century ballet masters advocated a "set" barre, that is, a series of exercises repeated daily with little variation. This tradition was continued well into this century by some teachers. Today, barre exercises more commonly are created anew for each class. Both "sides" have validity: a ritualized barre encourages strength, stamina, and perfection of material; a freshly created exercise series encourages quickness of perception, variety of muscle development, and responsiveness to the individual or class needs of a particular day.

Doubtless all would agree that some truth lies in both camps. Some of the benefits of both the "set" barre and the "varied" barre can be achieved by what could be termed the "progressive" barre. That is: establishing a consistent order of basic exercises to be followed for a series of classes, repeating two or three combinations for several lessons, and allowing one exercise to "lead" into the next, thus minimizing the explanation period between exercises. Following is an example of exercises leading into the one following:

A *BATTEMENT* SERIES

1. *Battement tendu* slowly to the front, returning to fifth position; repeat with a close to *demi-plié* in fifth position; remaining in *plié*, extend the foot again to the front; close to *demi-pointes* in fifth position; balance briefly, then lower

to *demi-plié*. Repeat all of the above, using the inside foot to extend to the back. Repeat again, using the outside foot to extend to the side (alternate closing back, front, back). Repeat once more to the side (alternate closing front, back, front) and, while in the balance on *demi-pointes*, make a *demi-détourné* (half-turn toward the back foot) to face the other side. Repeat the entire series to the new side.

2. Returning to the first side, continue with three *battements tendus* in moderate tempo to the front; *elevé* (rise to half-toe) in fifth position; lower to *demi-plié*. Repeat all, using the inside foot to extend to the back. Repeat, using the outside foot to extend to the side, alternating closings as in series 1. Repeat once more to the side, finishing with the *demi-détourné*. Lower to *demi-plié* and repeat series 2 to the new side.

3. Returning to the first side, continue by repeating all of series 2, closing each *battement tendu* in a *demi-plié* in fifth position. Perform this series to both sides.

4. Continue with eight quick *battements tendus* to the front with the accent on the close to fifth position. Repeat, using the inside foot to extend to the back. Repeat, using the outside foot to extend to the side (alternate closings) and quickly *elevé* and *demi-détourné* to the other side. Balance briefly before lowering to *demi-plié*. Repeat series 4 to the new side.

This series of *battements* is a fairly lengthy example of exercises related by a movement theme (straight *battements tendus* followed by those closing in *demi-plié*, followed by an *elevé* or rise to *demi-pointes*); a spatial pattern (to the front, to the back, to the side, and *demi-détourné*); a progression in tempi (from slow to moderate to quick); and a change of accent ("out" and "in," then just "in"). Because the combinations move logically along, they can be explained quickly and memorized easily. Portions of the same series could be repeated later with *battements dégagés* and again with *grands battements*.

Many other examples can be used: a *ronds de jambe* series progressing from *à terre* to *demi-grand en l'air* to *grand en l'air*; or *battements retirés* progressing to *attitudes* and then to *développés*. The important considerations are to have a consistent movement theme and spatial pattern with a progression, such as in tempi (from slow to quick) or in extension (from low to high).

One must keep in mind the reason for doing barre work in the first place: to warm up, limber, and strengthen the body, as well as discipline it for the varied demands of ballet. A highly inventive, constantly varied barre, requiring lengthy explanations and demonstrations, may thwart that goal. The completely set barre, utilizing the same muscles day after day, may be unrealistic, and uninspiring as well. The "progressive" exercise series is one answer to the dilemma.

A fitting conclusion to this discussion of barre work is the advice once more from August Bournonville:

Acquire early the habit of reflecting on your exercises, and you will save yourself needless exertion. It is not the quantity of exercises but their quality that ought to be considered.[4]

NOTES

1 Jack Anderson, *Dance* (New York: Newsweek Books, 1974), p. 48.

2 Raoul Gelabert, "Preventing Dancers' Injuries," *The Physician and Sportsmedicine*, Vol. 8, No. 4 (April 1980), p. 71.

3 *Ibid.*, pp. 71–72.

4 August Bournonville, *My Theatre Life*, trans. Patricia N. McAndrew (Middletown, Conn.: Wesleyan, 1979), p. 63.

CHAPTER THREE
CENTER
EXERCISES

*After the work at the barre, the
dancers moved to the center of the
floor to repeat exactly the same
exercises without holding on before
proceeding to the aplombs [balance
exercises].*

G. Léopold Adice, 1859.[1]

Today's dancers often are surprised to learn that yesterday's dancers of the nineteenth
and early twentieth centuries were expected to repeat *all* of their barre exercises in
center floor before continuing with the rest of the lesson. But today, the longer time
spent at barre has meant a shortened time allotted to center practice preceding
adagio or *pirouette* sequences. Frequently this means that only a single combination,
perhaps *battements tendus* with a few *relevés* or *pas de bourrées*, will be offered before
launching into more vigorous combinations. Yet, a few more minutes spent in a
simple series of center exercises provides a valuable period of transition from barre
work to floor work, a link between warm-up exercises and those requiring greater
dance awareness. Students who usually feel relatively secure at barre, but sometimes
apprehensive in center floor, are especially in need of that period of transition.
Indeed, all dancers benefit from three basic types of center exercises: those that
travel, turn, or change diagonal directions. In addition, center barre practice can
emphasize the use of *épaulement*, that important but often neglected coordination
of head and shoulder movements with the action of the legs. Although the concepts
of *épaulement* can be introduced during exercises at barre, they are particularly
relevant in the so-called traveling exercises.

44

Many barre exercises can be performed in center floor by alternating legs closing front, and thus traveling forward, or by alternating legs closing behind, and thus traveling backward. Although styles of *épaulement* vary, all apply the following basic concept for traveling exercises: the shoulder corresponding to the front leg is brought slightly forward, and the head turns and/or inclines toward that shoulder. A change of *épaulement* usually is made *as* the action of the working foot begins, if that foot is to change position from back to front, or from front to back. The *épaulement* thus established is held as the working foot closes to the new position. Many subtleties of *épaulement* have disappeared in contemporary choreography and thus have tended to be minimized in the classroom. For instance, a change of head and shoulder position can slightly precede the foot action, thus anticipating the new direction. Distinctions between turning of the head and the inclining of the head are not routinely observed, yet they can add beauty and elegance to the simplest of movement. Traditional* distinctions are:

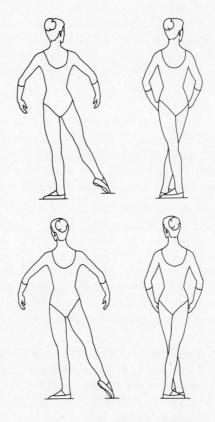

1. in steps traveling forward (or closing front), the head *turns* slightly in the direction of the working foot

2. in steps traveling backward (or closing back) the head *inclines* slightly away from the working foot

---

* In some styles the preference is for the head to both have a slight incline *and* turn toward the leg that is front.

In both cases, the movement of the head is toward the shoulder that is brought forward over the front leg.

The following traveling exercises are examples of center practice that can include concepts of *épaulement*. Traditionally, all begin in fifth position, right foot behind, *épaulement* toward the left.

BATTEMENTS

Description Without change of *épaulement*, *battement tendu à la seconde* with the right foot, then return it to fifth position behind. Changing the *épaulement* to the right, *grand battement à la seconde* with the right leg. Close the foot to fifth position front, keeping the *épaulement* to the right. Repeat the exercise using the left leg, changing the *épaulement* for the *grand battement*. After performing the series several times traveling forward, reverse the exercise, beginning with the left foot, and travel backward.

Note This particular combination of one *battement* without change of feet or *épaulement*, followed by one *battement* changing position, is particularly valuable as a preparation for many allegro combinations: *glissade derrière* followed by *jeté dessus*, or *glissade devant* followed by *assemblé dessous*, etc.

ROND DE JAMBE EN L'AIR

Description Changing the *épaulement* to the right, *dégagé* the left leg *à la seconde* at 45 degrees. *Rond de jambe en l'air en dehors* twice. Close the foot to fifth position back, keeping the *épaulement* to the right. Repeat the exercise using the right leg, changing the *épaulement* to the left. To reverse the series, begin with the right leg and perform *ronds de jambe en dedans*, closing front, *épaulement* toward the front leg.

**TURNING
EXERCISES**

Several exercises performed while making a quarter- or half-pivot can be valuable introductions to more complex *adagio* movements, as well as aids to better focus, coordination, and balance for turns. No *épaulement* is necessary for these exercises.

BATTEMENTS SOUTENUS EN TOURNANT

Description *Battement soutenu à la seconde* with the right foot, opening the arms to *demi-seconde*. Rise to fifth position *demi-pointes* by bringing the right foot directly front. Pivot on both feet, making a one-half-turn to the left as the arms close *demi-avant* (midway between *bras bas* and *bras avant*). The dancer now faces the back of the room, left foot front. From this position, *battement soutenu à la seconde* with the left foot, opening the arms to *demi-seconde*. Rise to fifth position *demi-*

pointes by bringing the left foot directly behind. Pivot on both feet, making one-half-turn to the left as the arms close. The dancer again faces the front of the room, right foot back.

Note When this exercise is performed slowly, the working leg usually travels to the side and returns to fifth position in a straight line each time, not by a circular route. However, with increased speed, and when performing a series of the turns, the leg may travel in a slightly circular pattern in order to increase momentum.

RONDS DE JAMBE À TERRE EN TOURNANT

Description To perform *en dehors*, begin with the right foot *pointe tendue derrière*. Pass the right foot forward through first position to *pointe tendue devant*. Make a quarter-pivot to the right on the left foot while circling the right foot through second position *pointe tendue* to *pointe tendue derrière*. Repeat the exercise three more times, finishing to the front of the room after one complete revolution.

To perform *en dedans*, reverse the action: pass the right foot through first position to *pointe tendue derrière*. Make a quarter-pivot to the left while circling the right foot through second position to *pointe tendue devant*. Continue as above, passing the foot backward through first position on each quarter-pivot.

Note The pivot is made on the whole of the supporting foot, but with the weight well forward over the ball of that foot, the heel only lightly touching the floor. To maintain the turnout of the supporting leg, keep the inside of that leg well forward and lengthened from heel to thigh.

DÉVELOPPÉ-ROTATION

Description From fifth position right foot front, *développé* forward to 45 degrees or 90 degrees *en l'air*, arms rising *en avant*. *Fondu* on the supporting leg, then *relevé* while making a quarter-pivot to the left, rotating the right leg in the hip socket and opening the arms *à la seconde*. Lower the left heel without changing the level of the extended right leg. The position of the body is now *à la seconde*, facing stage left. *Retiré* directly from the extended position, the arms closing *en bas*. Repeat the exercise three more times, finishing to the front of the room after one complete revolution. To reverse the exercise, *développé* with the right leg backward, and pivot to the right for each quarter-turn.

Note This exercise, also termed *battements divisés en quarts* (*battements* divided in fourths), is one of the first *adagios*, according to Agrippina Vaganova,[2] ballerina and later influential teacher in the U.S.S.R. Because it is a strenuous series, it should be performed on alternate legs before being reversed. That is, perform only four quarter-turns before changing to the other leg. Keep the arms well forward of the shoulders when opening them *à la seconde* during the pivot. Follow the general suggestions offered in Chapter 2 for *développé-rotation* at the barre.

DIAGONAL EXERCISES

Dancers at the intermediate level should already be acquainted with the positions of the body in space. The eight diagonal positions* require careful understanding of the relationship of the body to the front of the room as well as to the corners. They are illustrated here as seen from the back.

CROISÉ

ÉCARTÉ

DEVANT   DERRIÉRE   DEVANT   DERRIÉRE

EFFACÉ

ÉPAULÉ

DEVANT   DERRIÉRE   DEVANT   DERRIÉRE

For instance, the dancer should never face so much to the corner that the body appears in profile to most of the audience. Rather, the front of both shoulders and both hips should be visible from the front when the dancer stands in *croisé*, *écarté*, or *effacé* positions. This rule applies even when the dancer stands in fifth position facing toward downstage corners: the center of the body from the neck downward is aligned with the downstage corner of the dancer's "imaginary" stage square, not the actual corner of the room.

* Three more positions of the body, performed *en face*, are easier to master: *à la quatrième devant*, *à la quatrième derrière*, and *à la seconde* (shown on the following page as seen from the front).

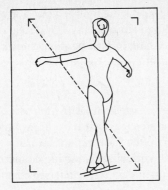

Exercises performed sequentially in selected diagonal positions are invaluable preparations for more complex center practice and *adagios*. The following combination is one such example.

The starting pose: fifth position *croisé* facing downstage left, *bras bas*. With the right foot, *battement tendu* forward, arms rising *en avant*. Hold the *pointe tendue* position as the arms open to *croisé devant*. Raise the leg to 45 degrees or 90 degrees, lower to *pointe tendue*, raise again, and then return the foot to fifth position as the high arm opens outward *à la seconde*. Both arms then close *en bas*. Repeat the sequence to *croisé derrière*, using the left leg. *Retiré* the right foot to the side of the supporting leg, arms rising *en avant*. *Développé* to *écarté devant*, arms opening to *écarté* simultaneously with the leg. Without changing the level of the extended leg, rotate to *effacé devant*, left arm rising *en haut* as the right arm lowers *à la seconde* and the body faces downstage right. *Fondu* on the left leg, then close the right foot to fifth position *demi-pointes* without otherwise changing the *effacé* position. *Pointe*

À LA QUATRIÈME
DEVANT

Á LA QUATRIÈME
DERRIÈRE

À LA SECONDE

tendue derrière with the left foot as the right leg lowers in *fondu* and the arms extend to *épaulé devant*. Remain in *fondu* and raise the left leg to 45 degrees or 90 degrees. *Pas de bourrée dessous*, finishing in fifth position *croisé* facing downstage right, as the arms close *en bas*. Repeat the exercise to the other side.

**CORPS
ET BRAS
COMBINATIONS**

One of the joys of intermediate ballet is the introduction to combinations—not just individual exercises or steps—which have been handed down through many ballet generations. Dancers often have certain favorites, perhaps a "set" *adagio* or *pirouette* series, which are particularly satisfying combinations of arm, leg, torso, and head movements. For many dancers, a preferred combination for center practice is *temps lié*.

TEMPS LIÉ (tahn-lee-AY)

Literally meaning linked time or movements, this venerable sequence, even in its simplest form, includes *demi-pliés* and *battements tendus* coordinated with *port de bras*, change of foot positions, and change of body direction. As might be expected, such a complex, popular exercise has many variants. The dancer constantly is reminded of the richness of the ballet "menu" and the subtle variations of "seasoning" within even the basic "dishes." The following description of *temps lié en avant* takes into account some of the possible variations of the exercise.

The starting pose: fifth position *croisé* facing downstage left, *bras bas*. *Demi-plié* and, as the arms rise *en avant*, either (A) *glissé* the front foot *en avant* (that is, remaining in *demi-plié*, glide forward to fourth position), or alternatively, (B) *pointe tendue devant* before shifting the weight forward to fourth position *demi-plié*. Transfer the weight entirely to the forward leg, straightening the knee, and extending the back foot to *pointe tendue derrière* as the arms open to *croisé devant*. Close the back foot to fifth position while either (A) immediately bending the knees in *demi-plié en face* as the raised arm lowers *en avant*, or alternatively, (B) retaining the *croisé* position of the body, and afterwards lower to *demi-plié en face* as above. From the *plié*, either (A) *glissé* the front (right) foot *à la seconde*, or alternatively, (B) *pointe tendue à la seconde*, and then shift the weight to second position *demi-plié* as the front (left) arm opens *à la seconde*. Transfer the weight to the leading (right) foot, straightening the knees, and extend the other foot to *pointe tendue à la seconde* as the head turns slightly in the direction of the pointed foot. As both arms close *en bas*, close the foot to fifth position front facing downstage right.

The exercise may finish with either (A) a *demi-plié* and incline of the head slightly away from the front foot, or alternatively, (B) straight legs in fifth position and the head turned in the direction of the front foot. Repeat the entire series to the other side, beginning toward downstage right. To perform *en arrière*, reverse the action by moving backward, then to the side by leading with the back foot, and close to fifth position behind. The (A) series is shown on page 51.

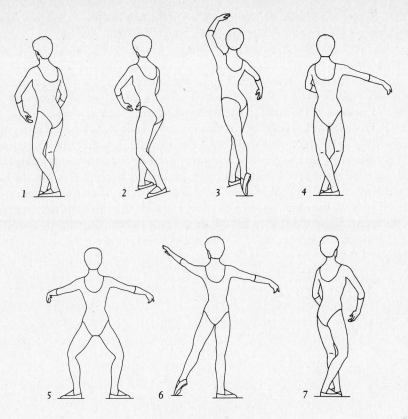

TEMPS LIÉ (example A)

Note   The primary difference in these two versions of *temps lié* is in the linking movement between the *demi-plié* in fifth position and the *pointe tendue* position *en croisé* or *à la seconde*. In version (A), the linkage is made by gliding through the open position *demi-plié*. In version (B), the linkage is made by extending the leading foot to *pointe tendue* before lowering it into the open position *demi-plié*. The quality of transfer of weight to the leading foot is crucial in both versions. It must be smooth and rhythmical, with a sense of continuity between each position. Therefore, the dancer should slightly anticipate the transfer of weight by directing the spine toward the leading foot before the heel of the other foot is allowed to release the floor.

MORE *CORPS ET BRAS* EXERCISES
Other combinations of *port de bras* include turning and bending the torso. Thus, the older term, *corps et bras*, is more apt because, in all of these examples, the spine,

chest, shoulders, and head are coordinated with the movements of the arms. Again, the combinations described here may have several different versions.

EXERCISE 1:

The starting pose: fifth position *croisé* facing downstage left, arms preparing from *en bas* through *en avant* to *croisé devant*, head inclined to the right. Open the left arm *à la seconde* as the head momentarily straightens, and immediately turn the torso as far to the left as possible, rotating from the waist so that the left arm moves backward while the right arm moves forward, head inclining to the right. The position of the torso, arms, and head is now *épaulé devant*. Lower both arms, bringing them to *demi-avant* as the head lowers slightly. Open the arms to *croisé devant* as the body resumes its original pose. Repeat the exercise twice more, then *pointe tendue à la seconde* with the back foot, opening the arms *à la seconde* as the body faces the front of the room. Close the foot to fifth position front in *demi-plié* facing downstage right, lowering the arms *en bas*. Straighten the knees, preparing the arms as above, and repeat the exercise to the other side.

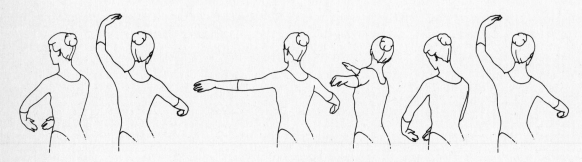

CORPS ET BRAS EXERCISE 1

Note In the method of Enrico Cecchetti, an eminent teacher of the late nineteenth and early twentieth centuries, there are eight exercises of *port de bras* that are performed in sequence. The exercise described above corresponds to the second *port de bras* of that series, with one important variation: instead of being in the *croisé devant* position, the arms in the Cecchetti exercise are in the Italian *attitude* position. Certain features remain constant, however: the strong turn from the waist does not affect the position of the hips, legs, or feet; the arms move from second position to *épaulé* because of the turn of the torso from the waist, a slight lift of the chest, and an intake of breath. In other words, the movement should flow in an organic, not arbitrary, manner.

EXERCISE 2:

The starting pose: fifth position *croisé* facing downstage left, arms preparing from *en bas* through *en avant* to *croisé derrière*, head inclined to the left. Change the arms to *croisé devant* position by changing the incline of the torso and head from left to right, simultaneously raising the left arm overhead and lowering the right arm *à la seconde*. Begin a half-circle of the torso: bend forward from the hip sockets, reaching the left arm as far as possible over the front foot; curve the spine as it bends lower and circles in front of the legs, closing the arms directly below the head and in front of the legs; continue to circle the torso slightly sideward toward the back foot, gradually lifting the spine to the upright position, opening the left arm *à la seconde* and raising the right arm overhead. The pose is once again *croisé derrière*. Repeat the exercise twice more, then *pointe tendue derrière* with the back foot, extending the right arm forward to *arabesque*, left arm extended backward (Russian fourth *arabesque*). *Fondu* on the supporting leg and immediately *pas de bourrée en dehors* to fifth position *croisé* facing downstage right, lowering the arms *en bas*. Prepare the arms as above and repeat the exercise to the other side.

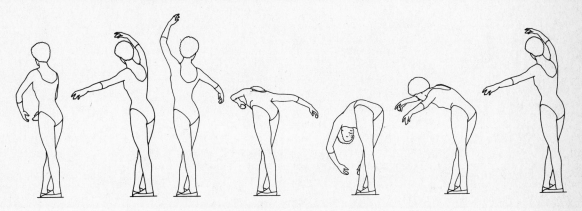

EXERCISE 2

Note Another version of this exercise calls for an immediate exchange of the arms at the lowest moment of the bend, rather than joining them below the head. In all versions, however, the dancer must "create the space" for the deep bend of the torso by lifting the abdominal muscles and lengthening the spine before the action begins. The strict vertical position of the legs can be maintained if the weight is kept well forward over the front of the feet, thus preventing the hips from pushing backward. As the arms circle, they must never fall behind the shoulders.

ADDITIONAL ARABESQUES (ah-ra-BESK) AND ATTITUDES (ah-tee-TEWD)

The *attitude* and *arabesque* are like the finest calligraphy—pristine and elegant, rapidly executed but carefully planned, seemingly effortless yet totally controlled, full of life and energy.
From a ballet student's essay, University of Hawaii, 1980.

Before considering additions to the basic *arabesques*, the dancer might reflect once again on the harmony of design and the counterbalancing of weight necessary for the correct execution of any *arabesque*. In general, the height of the forward arm should balance the height of the extended leg. Thus, the lower the leg, the higher the front arm. As the leg rises, the front arm moves into a more horizontal line. The back arm, usually slightly lower than the front arm, retains its relationship with the extended leg so that the important "negative space" (see Chapter 5) is never lost.

FIRST
(shown *à terre*)

SECOND
(shown *à la hauteur*)

RUSSIAN THIRD

and FOURTH

CECCHETTI THIRD
(shown on *demi-pointe*)

FOURTH

and FIFTH

ARABESQUES

As the leg rises, the pelvis responds by tilting slightly forward in order for the lower spine (lumbar vertebrae) to remain extended. A strong counter-pull now must be felt as the extended leg stretches backward from the pelvis and hip socket, while the torso stretches forward and upward through the upper spine (thoracic vertebrae) and head. A firm lift of the abdominal muscles again helps to create the space for the raised leg and to maintain the lift of the spine.

ARABESQUE ALLONGÉE (ah-ra-BESK ah-loh*n*-ZHAY)

Description   Although all *arabesques* involve an extended line, *arabesque allongée* means a particularly outstretched pose, in which the spine is less arched so that a straighter line can be drawn from the head to the toe of the extended leg. When performed *à terre*, the supporting knee is bent either *en fondu* or in a deep lunge. In either case, the weight is well lifted forward so that no pressure rests on the toe of the extended leg. When performed *à la hauteur*, the extended leg is raised to 90 degrees as the torso stretches forward from the hip socket, approximating a right angle to the supporting leg, which may remain straight or *en fondu*.

Note   The strong counter-pull of the leg and torso away from the hip sockets is especially important for the horizontal quality of *arabesque allongée*. Although the spine is less arched, it nevertheless maintains a strong lift, thus resisting any relaxation forward.

ARABESQUES ALLONGÉES

ARABESQUE PENCHÉE (ah-ra-BESK pah*n*-SHAY)

Description   In this leaning *arabesque*, the foot of the raised leg is the highest point of the pose, achieved by raising the leg so high that the torso must incline well forward from the hip socket. Although the spine does not straighten, as in *arabesque allongée*, it can extend slightly through the upper vertebrae and neck in order to counterbalance the height of the raised leg and also prevent tension in the head and shoulders. In *arabesques penchées*, the arms may have a variety of designs, but perhaps most commonly, they correspond to first or second *arabesque*. Thus, the hand of the forward arm appears to be in a direct line with the foot of the raised leg.

Note   In beginning any *penchée*, it is important to inhale, then allow the raised leg to initiate the forward incline of the torso, thus leading the action into the pose. In recovering from any *penchée*, the torso begins the lift upward, causing the leg to lower.

ARABESQUE PENCHÉE

In today's technique, with its emphasis on high leg extensions, *arabesque penchée* often resembles a vertical split. Although this is a logical outcome of the already extended design inherent in *arabesque penchée*, it should not sacrifice the harmony of a well-balanced and executed pose.

POSES *EN ATTITUDE*

The surprising variety of balletic styles that are both pleasing and proper is soon apparent when one considers poses *en attitude*. How high to lift the leg behind, how far forward to tilt the pelvis, how much to arch the spine, where to place the arms and focus the eyes, are just a few stylistic questions that have no one right answer. In general, it seems the older preference was for a lower leg and a more vertical, upright spine. Later versions required a higher lift of the thigh so that the lower leg, from knee to toe, could be parallel with the ground. In this position, the pelvis tilts slightly forward, the spine arches and lifts well upward from the waist. A more contemporary form allows an even greater tilt forward over the supporting leg so that the raised foot is as high as, or even higher than, the head. Today's dancer must be alert to these, and even more, variations of *attitude*, and be aware of which one is appropriate to use when performing in an early romantic style, a late-nine-teenth-century style, or a contemporary style. So too, the student must come to know what version of *attitude* is most convenient for turns or *allegro* steps, as well as for poses and *promenades*.

*ATTITUDE CROISÉE
DERRIÈRE*

ATTITUDE CROISÉE DERRIÈRE (ah-tee-TEWD krawh-ZAY deh-reeAIR)
Description Facing a downstage corner, stand on the leg nearest the audience and lift the other leg backward, its knee bent at a right angle and in line with the corresponding shoulder. In this position the calf and the foot of the raised leg,

crossed behind the dancer, are clearly visible from the front. Generally, the raised arm corresponds to the raised leg. The head may lift toward that high arm, or incline toward the audience.

Note Following the general rule for diagonal poses, *attitude croisée* requires a well-turned-out supporting leg, with both hips and shoulders facing toward the downstage corner of the room. To facilitate a high lift of the thigh, the dancer can inhale as the leg is raised, lifting the abdominal muscles and stretching the spine upward as the pelvis tilts slightly forward.

ATTITUDE CROISÉE DEVANT (ah-tee-TEWD krawh-ZAY duh-VAHn)

Description Facing a downstage corner, stand on the leg farthest from the audience and lift the other leg forward, knee half-bent and in line with the corresponding shoulder, the raised foot in line with the opposite shoulder. The spine remains vertical while the foot of the raised leg is lifted as high as possible. The arms may be *en haut* with either or both arms raised, or in some other pleasing position.

*ATTITUDE CROISÉE
DEVANT*

ATTITUDE EFFACÉE DERRIÈRE (ah-tee-TEWD eh-fah-SAY deh-reeAIR)

Description Facing a downstage corner, stand on the leg farthest from the audience and raise the other leg backward, knee half-bent so the lower part of the leg and the raised foot are clearly visible to the audience. The torso may incline forward or remain upright, depending upon stylistic preferences and also upon the height of the raised leg. Usually the raised arm corresponds to the raised leg. Typically this pose is not performed *devant*, and therefore it is simply known as *attitude effacée*.

ATTITUDE EFFACÉE DERRIÈRE

57

ATTITUDE DE FACE (ah-tee-TEWD duh FAHSS)

Description Facing directly to the front of the room, raise either leg to the back, the knee well bent at a right angle and in line with the corresponding shoulder so that the raised foot, crossed behind, is visible from the front. The arms may be slightly forward of second position (*demi-bras au public*), or the raised arm may correspond to the raised leg.

ATTITUDE DE FACE

ATTITUDE À TERRE (ah-tee-TEWD ah TAIR)

Description Facing a downstage corner, stand on the leg nearest the audience and bend the other leg, foot pointed on the ground either directly behind the supporting ankle or crossed behind the opposite shoulder. One arm may be *en haut* and the other *en avant*.

ATTITUDE À TERRE

A rich assortment of material to combine in *adagio* sequences is available for even the elementary student: *grands* and *demi-pliés*, *relevés*, *développés*, various *battements*, *ronds de jambe*, *attitudes*, *arabesques*, and preparations for *pirouettes*. The intermediate student may choose exercises from an even larger array, including many of the barre exercises described in the previous chapter, such as *grands ronds de jambe à terre* and *en l'air*, *développé-rotations*, *développé en fondu*, and the various *cambrés*. To this sizeable list now can be added several exercises combining the essential elements of harmony of design, flow of movement, and controlled balance, which characterize an *adagio* sequence.

PROMENADE (prawm-NAHD)

Description   To present a pose *en promenade* is to maintain a certain position, such as second *arabesque*, while slowly revolving in one spot (*sur place*) on the supporting foot. The pivot is made on the ball of the foot by ever so slightly lifting and moving the heel. These almost imperceptible heel movements allow the dancer to smoothly revolve either *en dehors* (toward the raised leg) or *en dedans* (toward the supporting leg). Any of the *arabesques*, *attitudes*, and positions of the body can be performed *en promenade*.

Note   The pivoting action of the supporting foot can be practiced with quarter- or half-revolutions while maintaining the raised leg at *demi-hauteur*, or even lower, before the complete turn is tried with full extension. Five essential requirements must obtain when the dancer, balanced over one leg, displays a pose *en promenade*:

1. Both the supporting leg and the extended leg remain well turned-out so that the design of the pose never becomes overly crossed or opened.
2. The supporting heel retains its alignment with the rest of the foot so that it never twists or sickles.
3. The hips and shoulders remain in alignment, squarely facing each new direction as the pivot is made.
4. The spine retains the shape of the pose so that the arms do not alter as the *promenade* is made. This obtains unless an alteration of pose is required, such as a change from *arabesque* to *attitude* during the *promenade*, or unless a stylistic preference is designated, such as the turning inward of the forward hand during some pivots in *arabesque*.
5. The eyes focus clearly on each new direction as the pivot is made.

DÉTOURNÉ D'ADAGE (day-toor-NAY dah-DAZH)

Description   Combining elements of *promenade* and *rotation*, *détourné d'adage* is a pivot on one foot in which the body turns to face the leg which was behind. For instance, from the pose *quatrième derrière*, left leg extended behind, the dancer makes one quarter-turn to the left on the flat of the right foot as the raised leg rotates in the hip socket to second position, body facing stage left. Without pause, the dancer continues to turn to face upstage as the raised leg rotates to *quatrième devant*. The turn is then completed by a *promenade* in that pose, left leg extended front.

The change of pose while rotating from *croisé derrière* to *croisé devant* is particularly beautiful. Sometimes called *dégagé en tournant* (Cecchetti method), this pivot is made by a half-turn *en dehors*, rotating the raised leg through second position to *quatrième devant*, followed by a *promenade* in the new position to *croisé devant*. Thus, if the dancer begins facing downstage left (*en croisé derrière*), the rotation is made as the dancer turns to face upstage left (in second position), then upstage right (*en quatrième devant*), and the *promenade* continues the turn to downstage right, finishing in *croisé devant*.

The dancer can, of course, begin the exercise with one leg extended forward, making the turn in the direction of the supporting leg as the extended leg rotates to the back.

DÉTOURNÉ D'ADAGE

Note Although the raised leg rotates in the hip socket, it does so because of the turn of the body. Indeed, for the observer, the beauty of this exercise is the apparent suspended immobility of the raised leg. For the performer, the pleasure of any *détourné d'adage* is the awareness of the spine that comes during the changes of pose, made possible, in part, by the strong lift of the abdominal muscles throughout the exercise.

**SOME
FOUETTÉS**
(fweh-TAY)

The term *fouetté* applies to a great variety of ballet steps and usually implies a strong whipping action of the foot or leg. Perhaps the best known of the *fouetté* family are *fouetté rond de jambe en tournant* (commonly referred to as *fouetté* turn) and *grand fouetté en tournant* (in which the dancer makes a whole turn *en l'air* or *en relevé* while executing a *grand battement* followed by a rotation of the body).

Exciting steps, yes, but often frustrating because they usually are beyond the technical range of the intermediate student. The following *fouetté* "cousins" perhaps are more appropriate as first *fouetté* acquaintances—certainly they are important *adagio* exercises in their own right. (Please also refer to Chapters 4 and 6 for yet more members of the *fouetté* family.)

DEMI-FOUETTÉ (d'mee fweh-TAY)
Description   From fifth position *en face*, raise the right leg 90 degrees *à la seconde* by making a *grand battement* or *développé*. Quickly turn the body to *arabesque* on the left foot as the right leg rotates in the hip socket. The pose is now in profile to the audience.

Note   The exercise can be learned with the sole of the supporting foot on the floor, but later it is done with a *relevé*. After the *fouetté* to *arabesque*, the heel lowers, and then the supporting knee can *fondu*.

DEMI-FOUETTÉ

Carefully synchronized *port de bras* enhances any *fouetté* movement. For this exercise, the dancer can raise both arms *en avant* then *en haut* as the leg is raised *à la seconde*. From there the arms open sharply to first *arabesque* as the body makes the quarter-turn. It is important that the elbows open strongly outward to the *arabesque* pose, never dropping or falling inward toward the body during the rotation. The extension (not tension!) of the pose should be reflected right through to the fingertips of both hands.

FOUETTÉ EN RELEVÉ (fweh-TAY ahn ruh-leh-VAY)
Description   This exercise has a variety of names (including *grand fouetté en tournant*) and also some variety of execution. One of the simplest, although by no

means easy, versions is the following: from first *arabesque* facing stage right, pass the back leg forward through first position *demi-plié* and make a *grand battement devant en relevé*, still in profile to the audience. As soon as the leg reaches its full height in the *battement*, make a sharp half-turn *en demi-pointe*, the leg rotating in the hip socket to first *arabesque* facing stage left. Lower the heel and *fondu* on the supporting leg. The exercise can be repeated, thus finishing in the starting pose facing stage right.

FOUETTÉ EN RELEVÉ

Another version of *fouetté en relevé* begins with a step, usually as the body turns to face an upstage corner, before the leg passes through first position to *grand battement devant*. The half-turn then is made to *arabesque fondu* facing the opposite downstage corner.

Note For intermediate technique, it is important that the spine be held firmly upright as the *grand battement* is made, unlike the more advanced version in which the body is allowed to tilt slightly backwards. The final *arabesque* pose requires that the pelvis tilt slightly forward in order to allow the leg to remain at the same level as in the *battement devant*. Hips and shoulders must squarely face each new direction, necessitating careful execution and timing of the *port de bras:* lower the arms *en bas* as the leg passes through first position *demi-plié*, then raise the arms *en avant* before *en haut* during the *grand battement*; open the arms sharply outward to *arabesque* as the turn is made. (Please refer to the section on *développé-rotation* in the previous chapter for discussion of the use of breath and muscle coordination applicable to *fouettés* as well.)

PETIT FOUETTÉ (p'tee fweh-TAY)

Description This small whipped movement usually comes in pairs and often goes by the name flic-flac (fleek-FLAK), a term of the Russian method. From second position *dégagé*, brush the pointed toes sharply inward along the ground, crossing just beyond the front of the supporting ankle (*petit fouetté devant*). Immediately fling the foot again to second position, without brushing the floor. Repeat the movement, but this time cross the foot just beyond the back of the supporting ankle (*petit fouetté derrière*). To reverse the exercise, begin *derrière* and finish *devant*. The second *petit fouetté* may finish with a rise to *demi-pointe*.

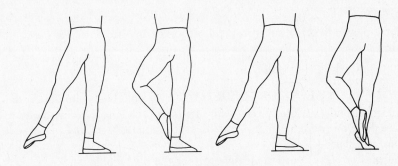

PETIT FOUETTÉ

Note *Petits fouettés* or flic-flac can be used as connecting movements in center exercises or *adagio* sequences. For instance, following a *développé à la seconde*, the leg can be lowered for quick *petits fouettés devant* and *derrière* before being raised to *attitude croisée derrière*. In later stages of training, the movement also is made with a full turn either *en dehors* (brush *derrière* and then turn *en relevé* toward the working leg as it whips *devant*) or *en dedans* (brush *devant* and then turn *en relevé* toward the supporting leg as the working foot whips *derrière*).

Some common distinctions used in describing turning steps are:

Tourner (toor-NAY): to turn around or revolve.

En tournant (ahn toor-NAHn): turning while performing a step (such as *pas de bourrée en tournant*).

Tour (toor): a turn in the air, or on half or full point after a *piqué*.

Pirouette (peer-ooWET): a turn on one foot after a *relevé*.

The following discussion can treat only briefly a few of the important turns for the intermediate student. Some other steps performed *en tournant* are described in the following chapter. Important general observations include: attention to the rhythm of the turn and the correct carriage of the head. Indeed, understanding the fundamental rhythmic structure of any ballet step is a primary key to understanding the step itself. Turns may be done sharply and quickly, as in *allegro* combinations, or smoothly and slowly, as in *adagio* sequences. Equally important for all basic turns are the carriage of the head and the focus of the eyes. The head remains upright, never tilted, with the eyes focused on one spot at eye level. As the turn begins, the eyes momentarily remain focused on the spot, then during the turn the head turns quickly so that the eyes can focus again on their spot.

Four phases of each turn will be described here:

1. The preparation,
2. The initiative or action leading into the turn,
3. The turn itself,
4. The completion.

These phases typically occur in rapid succession but are separated here for the sake of clarity.

PIQUÉ (or POSÉ) TOUR EN DEDANS (pee-kay TOOR ahn duh-DAHn)

Students usually are introduced to this turn after becoming acquainted with turns that are done on two feet (such as *soutenus en tournant en dedans* and *en dehors*, *chaînés*, and *tours de basque*).

Preparation   For a turn to the right, extend the right foot forward while making a *fondu* on the supporting leg. At the same time, turn the head toward the right shoulder and raise to *demi-avant* the arm corresponding to the forward leg and the other arm to *demi-seconde*.

Initiative   Keeping the right leg straight and foot pointed, swing it to second position (as in a *demi-rond de jambe en dehors*) and, with a strong push from the supporting foot, immediately face the right leg and step directly onto *demi-pointe*, knee straight. At the same time, open the right arm slightly and raise the left foot *sur le cou-de-pied derrière* (in back of the right ankle) or to *retiré derrière* (behind, or just below, the back of the right knee).

Turn   Without pause, execute a three-quarter turn *en dedans* to the right while closing the arms to *demi-avant*. During the spin, the head faces briefly toward the left shoulder, then quickly resumes its focus over the right shoulder.

Completion   *Coupé dessous* with the left foot. At the same time, quickly extend the right leg forward, keeping the knee straight and the toes only a few inches above the ground, and open the left arm to *demi-seconde*. The position now is the same as the preparatory one.

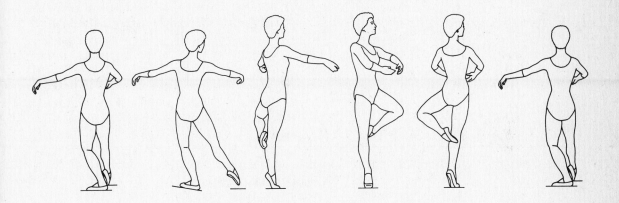

PIQUÉ TOUR EN DEDANS

Note   Variations of this basic turn involve variation in the positions of the raised leg and the arms. During the spin, the raised leg may be brought to the front of the supporting ankle or knee, lifted to *attitude*, or extended to *arabesque*, and the arms may be raised to a corresponding complementary position. During the *coupé* following the spin, the supporting foot may release *sur le cou-de-pied devant* before extending for the preparation of another turn.

Often *piqué tours* occur in a series done diagonally across the room. Later they can be done circling the floor. As in any turn, the *piqué tour* may be a multiple spin. When more than a single turn is attempted, it is helpful to inhale as the turns begin, lift the abdominal muscles strongly as the arms close swiftly, and spot the head more rapidly. Care should be taken always to open and close the arms along an even line so that the leading arm does not "pump" up and down. Of course, when the turn is made in a particular pose, such as *attitude derrière*, it requires the arms assume a complementary position as the turn is made.

PIQUÉ TOUR EN DEHORS (pee-kay TOOR ahn duh-OHR)
Preparation   For a turn to the right, the same preparation may be taken as for the *tour en dedans* described above.

Inititative   Carry the right leg to second position and immediately *fondu* on it. At the same time open the arms to *demi-seconde* and point the left foot *à la seconde*. Cross the left foot directly in front of the right and step onto the left *demi-pointe* as the arms begin to close.

PIQUÉ TOUR EN DEHORS

Turn   Without pause, raise the right foot *sur le cou-de-pied devant* or to *retiré devant* and turn to the right, closing the arms to *demi-avant*. The head spots as previously described.

Completion   *Fondu* on the left leg, and open the left arm *demi-seconde*. If the *tour en dehors* is to be repeated, then, instead of the *fondu* on the left leg, immediately *tombé à la seconde* onto the right leg and continue as above.

Note   The *tour* just described travels to the side, but another variation can be performed *sur place: dégagé* the left foot *à la seconde*, cross the left foot in front of the right, step onto the left *demi-pointe*, and turn to the right with the right foot raised *devant*. To complete this *tour*, *coupé dessus* with the right foot and extend the left foot *à la seconde*.

In both the basic *piqué tour en dehors* and *en dedans*, it is important that the raised foot be placed quickly and firmly in position against the supporting leg for the duration of the turn.

PIROUETTE EN DEHORS (peer-oo-WET ahn duh-OHR)

Having learned and practiced exercises that combine elements of the *pirouette*—*demi-plié*, *relevé*, and balance on one foot with coordinated arm movement—students are ready for the study of the *pirouette* itself. It may be taken from a *demi-plié* in either second, fourth, or fifth position, and it is wise to get acquainted with all three possibilities, for each has merit. Indeed, if problems of balance occur—and they inevitably do for almost every dancer—they sometimes are resolved by a change of the preparatory *plié*. Both second and fourth positions allow for a strong push-off, enabling the dancer to achieve multiple *pirouettes* more easily than from fifth position. However, fifth position provides a more central base from which to *relevé* and is effective for the execution of a series of rapid single *pirouettes*. In a preparation from second position, the dancer can more easily square the hips and shoulders to the front direction, but a preparation from fourth position allows the dancer to anticipate the supporting leg by the slight forward shift of weight during the *demi-plié*. The great ballerina and teacher Tamara Karsavina offers this suggestion for finding the correct stance in a preparation from fourth position:

> To know how the weight should be distributed in any individual case it is useful to make the pupil take the preparation, then raise slightly the back foot off the ground while remaining in *demi-plié* on the front foot. If the position thus can be sustained this means the distribution is correct.[3]

The wise lady hints at another important consideration for *pirouettes*: the individuality of each performer. One dancer may turn brilliantly to the left, but with trepidation to the right. Another may prefer a quick preparatory step, such as *pas de bourrée en tournant*, before a *pirouette*. The height of the raised leg (*sur le cou-de-pied devant* to *retiré devant*) and the position of the ball of the supporting foot on the floor (quarter-point, half-point, three-quarter-point) are more than stylistic differences; they also reflect different individual needs for better balance and control, especially when learning *pirouettes*. Once again, exact rules are hard to codify, for many correct answers exist. The student must become acquainted with the choices available and learn which are most compatible with his or her physique and technical development. The performer, of course, must be prepared to meet the requests of a choreographer.

Thus, the following description of *pirouette en dehors* represents only one of several choices that might be attempted.

Preparation For a turn to the right, *pointe tendue à la seconde* with the right foot, raising the arms *en avant* and then opening them *à la seconde*. *Demi-plié* in either second position, fourth position back, or fifth position front, taking care that the open positions are relatively small and that the closed position is not over-crossed. During the *demi-plié* the right arm may be brought *en avant* or may slightly cross the center of the body so that the elbow is more rounded than usual.

Initiative Open the right arm slightly to the side and, with a firm push from the right foot, *relevé* on the left foot, bringing the right foot *sur le cou-de-pied devant* or to *retiré devant*. The body has now made an eighth of a turn to the right, but the head remains focused front.

Turn Without pause, execute a three-quarter turn to the right, closing the arms swiftly to *demi-avant* and snapping the head quickly around to regain the front focus. The raised foot remains securely placed against the supporting leg.

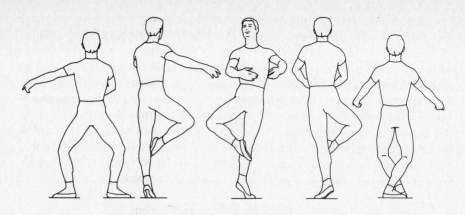

PIROUETTE EN DEHORS

Completion   Lower the supporting heel, then lower the raised foot to fifth position back in *demi-plié*. (See below for alternate closings.)

Note   Confusion sometimes arises concerning the direction of the turn when the preparation can be taken from so many different positions. The rule for *pirouette en dehors* is: turn toward the leg that is raised.

Correct timing of all the elements of the turn is essential for the success of the turn itself. This is easier said than done, and accordingly *pirouettes* require patient practice. The force for the spin comes from the strong push-off from the *plié* and the swift closing of the arms. Then, an intake of breath seems to help stabilize and suspend the body. This intake of breath is especially important for multiple spins, as is the rapid spotting of the head and the clear focus of the eyes.

Pirouettes en dehors usually finish by closing the raised foot behind the supporting leg. This may be achieved in a variety of ways in addition to the one described above: spring simultaneously to both feet in fifth position *demi-plié*, spring to a small fourth position *demi-plié*, or *fondu* on the supporting leg as the raised foot is lowered to fourth position in back with the knee straight and the sole of the foot on the floor. In all cases, the complete turn must be executed before the raised foot begins to lower. Indeed, in some instances it does not lower at all after the turn, but instead extends to a desired pose *à la hauteur* as the supporting heel lowers. After rapid spins it is helpful to open the arms swiftly in order to halt the momentum of the turn. For *adagio* turns, the arms may remain closed at the completion of the turns, or they may open slowly to the desired position.

PIROUETTE EN DEDANS (peer-oo-WET ahn duh-DAHn)

Although the preparation for *pirouette en dedans* can be taken from a variety of positions, it perhaps is easiest from fourth position, either with *demi-plié*, or, more commonly, with only a *fondu* on the forward leg. Usually the preparation is made toward the downstage corner of the room, the dancer standing either *croisé* or *effacé* to the audience. The former is described here.

Preparation   For a turn to the right, *pointe tendue croisé devant* with the right foot, raising the arms *en avant*. Lower the heel and *fondu* on the right leg, shifting the weight forward over that leg while keeping the left leg straight with the sole of the foot on the ground. During the *fondu*, open the left arm *à la seconde* and curve the right elbow more than usual. Focus directly to the front of the room.

Initiative   Swing the left leg *à la seconde* at 45 degrees, facing the front of the room and opening the right arm *à la seconde*. Immediately *relevé* on the right foot and simultaneously whip the extended foot to the supporting leg, touching the left toe just below the right knee. At the same time, close the arms swiftly to *demi-avant*. The body now faces the right downstage corner of the room, but the focus of the head remains front.

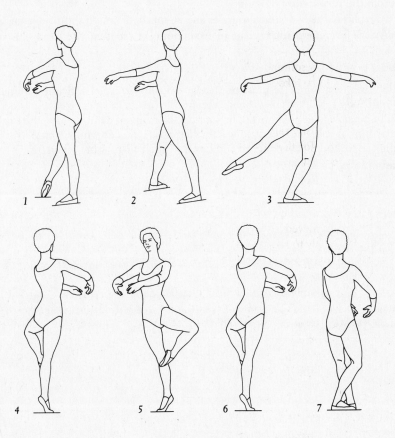

PIROUETTE EN DEDANS

Turn   Without pause, execute a full turn to the right, snapping the head quickly around to regain the front focus.

Completion   Lower both feet simultaneously to fifth position *demi-plié*, keeping the left foot front. The body is now in *croisé* to the downstage right corner. (See below for alternate closings.)

Note   The direction of a turn *en dedans* is always toward the supporting leg. Usually *pirouettes en dedans* finish with the raised foot in front, either in fifth position, as described above, or in a *tombé en avant* or in a *coupé dessus*. Later, the finish may be taken with a *fondu* on the supporting leg as the raised leg is extended to any desired position *à la hauteur*.

The initiative for the turn does not always require a *dégagé* or swing of the leg *à la seconde*, as described above. Instead, from a *demi-plié* in fourth or fifth position, the back foot can be brought directly to the front of the supporting leg during the *relevé*. In this case, the arms usually do not open to the side, but rise directly *en haut* from the preparatory position.

A strong lift of the abdominal muscles and an intake of breath should accompany the *relevé*. The neck must remain relaxed, however, so that the head can spot efficiently.

And it is well to be reminded that:

> The finish of a *pirouette* must be steady and self-possessed with the outline of your body and limbs correct and graceful. To obtain the most pleasing effect it is impossible to exaggerate the importance of spinning daintily upon the toe, as nothing is more repellent to watch than a bad dancer who keeps shifting from toe to heel and jerking up and down in each turn of his *pirouette*.
> Carlo Blasis, 1820.[4]

NOTES

1 G. Léopold Adice, *Théorie de la Gymnastique de la Dance Théâtrale* (Paris, 1859). Partial translation by Leonore Loft in Selma Jeanne Cohen, *Dance as a Theatre Art* (New York: Dodd, Mead, 1974), p. 74.

2 Agrippina Vaganova, *Basic Principles of Classical Ballet* (Leningrad, 1934). Translation by Anatole Chujoy (New York: Dover, 1969), p. 38.

3 Tamara Karsavina, *Ballet Technique* (New York: Theatre Arts Books, 1956). p. 19.

4 Carlo Blasis, *An Elementary Treatise Upon the Theory and Practice of the Art of Dancing* (Milan, 1820). Translation by Mary Stewart Evans (New York: Dover, 1968), p. 50.

CHAPTER FOUR
ALLEGRO

But I shall be told that a person has no bent for dancing; to which I reply we can always learn when we wish to do so. . . . Dancing is no more than knowing how to bend and straighten the knees at the proper time.

Pierre Rameau, 1725.[1]

The intermediate student must jump both higher and quicker, smoother and sharper, with more changes of direction and *port de bras* than the elementary student. The fun and frustration of such *allegro* steps, especially when linked in combinations, daily assail the dancer, who must remember that

> Natural elevation is a boon accorded to the few only; but where it is not granted by nature it can be developed by a systematic, well-planned training.[2]

And where there is the wish to learn, one will do so. Frequently this may mean a return to concentrated practice of more elementary steps and exercises, a going backward before continuing forward. Therefore, although *allegro* steps beyond the basic ones are the primary concerns of this chapter, they in no way replace methodical practice of those fundamental jumps, leaps, and hops whose very nature depends upon the correctly executed *demi-plié* and push from the floor, the "knowing how to bend and straighten the knees at the proper time," as dancing master Pierre Rameau observed over 250 years ago.

A series of elementary *allegro* steps that alternate the manner of push-off (from both feet or from one foot) and the manner of landing (on both feet or on one foot) are valuable both as preparatory and as strengthening exercises for more complicated *allegro*. Examples of some combinations are:

1. *Sauté* four times in first position,
   sissonne simple with the right foot *devant* just above and in front of the left ankle,
   assemblé to first position,
   sissonne simple with the left foot *devant*,
   assemblé to first position.
   Repeat the entire combination with *sissonnes simples derrière*.

2. *Sauté* in the first position,
   sissonne simple devant,
   temps levé without changing the position of the raised foot,
   assemblé to first position.
   Repeat the entire combination to the other side and then with *sissonnes simples derrière*.

Allegro steps vary enormously, not only in their basic designs but also in their inherent dynamic qualities. This is obvious when a *terre à terre* step such as *glissade* is compared to a step of high elevation, such as *grand jeté*. But sometimes it is not so obvious when a *glissade* is performed just before or after a step of lower elevation, such as *petit jeté*. Too often characteristics particular to each step become common to both, and thus dynamic contrasts are lost. This failure frequently is attributable to lack of rhythmic understanding and to the use made of that all-important *demi-plié*, both before and after the step. The bend of the knees both for take-off and landing will vary in depth and quality depending upon the sequence of steps and the speed and dynamics of the music. A dancer can learn to adjust the character of the *demi-plié*, and thus also the rebound into the air, in relatively simple exercises. For example, a series of *changements de pieds* done to a moderate 4/4 rhythm, necessitating deep *demi-pliés*, can then be repeated to a lively 6/8 rhythm (perhaps a gigue or tarantella), thus calling for shorter, or quarter-*pliés*.

Some suggestions of other elementary exercises utilizing variations in the character of the *plié* and the rebound into the air are:

1. Eight *sautés* in first position with the accent on the landing, immediately followed by eight more *sautés* with the accent on the rebound into the air. Repeat the exercise.

In order to change the accent from down to up, the dancer must make an especially deep bend of the knees following the eighth *sauté*. Similarly, in order to change the accent from up to down, the dancer can sustain the last *sauté* in the air by inhaling and raising the arms from a lower to higher position. Further challenges occur by reducing the series to four or two of each type of *sauté*, the combination repeated then for sixteen or thirty-two counts.

2. *Changement* quickly three times (count *one and two*),
   sissonne simple devant (count *and three*),
   assemblé devant (count *and four*).
   Repeat the *changements, sissonne,* and *assemblé* to the other side, then repeat the entire combination with *sissonnes* and *assemblés derrière*.

The first two *changements* need shorter *demi-pliés* than the third. Thus, the stronger push-off after the last *changement* makes the *sissonne* the dynamic highlight of the combination, followed by the relatively weaker push-off from one foot for the *assemblé*.

More discussion of rhythm and dynamics will follow. But now it is time to single out for discussion some of the *allegro* steps that make up the intermediate technical repertory. They will be grouped according to size—small, medium, and large steps—and to general characteristics, such as steps that are primarily connecting movements, or that turn, or that have beats.

CONNECTING AND/OR PREPARATORY STEPS

Many steps can be used to connect to or prepare for others, but some steps are used almost exclusively in these functions. The success of *allegro* combinations often depends upon the careful execution of these small steps. Above all, these preparatory or connecting steps must be properly timed, be rhythmically correct, in order to serve their purpose. Two common steps in this category are *glissade* and *pas de bourrée*, counted respectively, *"and one"* (*glissade*) and *"and a one"* (*pas de bourrée*). When these steps lead to a large jump or leap, they need not finish in fifth position, but may go through and slightly beyond that position (into a small over-crossed fourth position) *if* care is taken to keep the legs well turned-out. For intermediate technique, other types of *glissade* and *pas de bourrée* also are useful:

GLISSADE PRÉCIPITÉE (glee-SAHD pray-see-pee-TAY)
This very quick, or accelerated, *glissade* occurs before the musical beat so that the ensuing step, usually a *posé (piqué)*, can occur on the downbeat. Together, the *glissade précipitée* and *posé* are counted *"and one"*; thus this *glissade* is twice as quick, and usually twice as small, as an ordinary one. It can be done in any direction—forward, backward, or to the side.

Description   To perform one example of *glissade précipitée en avant*, begin in fifth position right foot front, facing the *effacé* direction (downstage right). Make a quarter-*plié* and quickly brush the right foot forward as in a *battement dégagé*. Without any pause, spring forward off the left foot, allowing the toes of the right foot to then touch the ground only a fraction of a second before the left foot closes to it. Quickly lower to quarter-*plié*, and, if a *posé* is to follow the *glissade*, again extend the right leg forward and immediately push from *fondu* on the left leg to *demi-pointe* on the right. The left leg will raise to the desired position, perhaps *arabesque* or *attitude*.

Note The arms play an important role in such a quick preparatory step as this one. Because the following movement typically is a larger one, thus requiring more open or extended arms, the small *glissade précipitée* tends to have the arms curved inward toward the body so that they may then release outward to establish the next pose.

PAS DE BOURRÉE COURU (pah duh boo-RAY koo-REW)

This is a running step of three movements, not to be confused with another sequence often going under the same name (or sometimes simply called *bourrée couru*) that has rapid but tiny multiple steps on *pointe* or *demi-pointe* traveling in a close fifth or parallel first position. By contrast, the version described below allows the dancer to make a healthy, but carefully controlled, three-step run in anticipation of a larger movement, usually a leap or jump that may even turn in the air. This *bourrée* has several advantages over other preparatory steps: it enables the dancer to cover a great deal of space, it helps build momentum to send the body higher and farther in the air, and, coupled with the ensuing leap, it creates a vision of lightness.

Description To perform *pas de bourrée couru en avant* (perhaps preparing for a *grand jeté* forward), begin in *croisé* with the right foot at *pointe tendue* behind. *Fondu* on the left leg as the right makes a *petit développé* forward. With a push from the *fondu*, step well forward onto the right foot, quickly descending through the instep, and then forward onto the left foot. Without pause, step out again onto the right foot, this time into a deep *fondu*. Immediately push from the ground into the *grand jeté* (or whatever desired step). These three forward steps occur quickly and without interruption as a three-step run, the final step having a strong bend of the knee.

To perform *pas de bourrée couru en arrière* (perhaps preparing for a "*tour jeté*"), begin in the same *croisé* position, right foot behind. *Fondu* deeply on the left leg, allowing the right foot to lift slightly off the floor and reach farther backward. Push from the *fondu*, stepping backward as far as the right foot will reach. The body will turn slightly to the right on this first step of the *bourrée*. Allow the left foot then to cross in front and beyond the right foot on the second step (closing to fifth position would halt the momentum of the run), and quickly step out into *fondu* on the right foot, heel well pressed into the floor. The body will turn quickly in the direction of this forward step, the result being a half-turn to the right during this three-step ·sequence.

Note Each movement of the *bourrée* requires careful use of the insteps so that the feet contact the floor toe first, *never* heel first. The body must anticipate the direction the steps will travel so that the weight never falls behind the moving foot. Indeed, in the final step, the body must be especially well over the leg in *fondu*, the

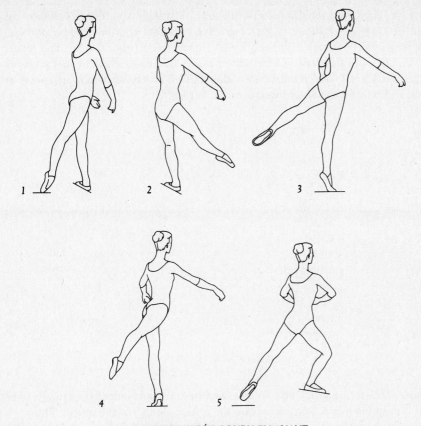

PAS DE BOURRÉE COURU EN AVANT

weight actually slightly forward of the supporting foot. As the *pas de bourrée couru* begins, the arms often open outward to help start the momentum, then close quickly during the final two steps in order to extend to the desired position during the following leap or jump.

DEMI-CONTRETEMPS (d'mee-kahn-truh-TAHN)

Another useful preparation for a larger movement is *demi-contretemps*, composed of a *sissonne simple* (or a *temps levé*) followed by a *glissé* (also called *chassé*). The momentum generated by this combination of springing and sliding movements can propel the body both upward and outward in space during the following step, perhaps a *grand assemblé porté*.

Description   To perform *demi-contretemps en avant* (the usual direction of the step), begin in fifth position *croisé* right foot front. *Sissonne simple*, that is, *demi-plié* and push from both feet upward and forward into the air, quickly raising the back foot *sur le cou-de-pied derrière* as the body turns slightly to the right to face the *effacé* direction. (The step may begin with the back foot at *pointe tendue derrière*. If so, *fondu* on the front leg, lifting the back leg to a low *attitude derrière*, and *temps levé*, that is, push from the front leg into the air, turning to *effacé* as above.) Land on the right leg in *fondu*, immediately sliding the left foot forward to fourth position *croisé*, and transfer the weight well over the left leg.

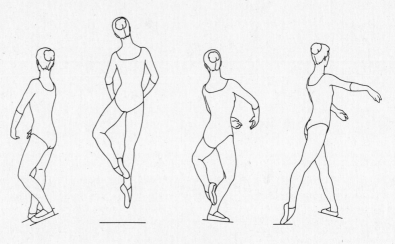

DEMI-CONTRETEMPS

Note   The term *contretemps* implies "against time," and indeed the initial movement, the spring into the air, occurs on the upbeat ("*and*") of the music. This very moment is distinctive for the *demi-contretemps* because of the pose in the air: the body has turned from *croisé* to *effacé*, the back foot is held firmly *sur le cou-de-pied derrière* against the forward leg, the arms are *en bas*, and the head inclines toward the downstage shoulder.

FAILLI (fi-YEE)

Similar to *demi-contretemps*, and sometimes confused with it, is *failli*, used often as a preparatory movement for steps with beats. It begins in fifth position and consists of a *sissonne ouverte en avant* followed by a *glissé* or *chassé en avant*.

Description   *Failli* has two acceptable versions, and thus two possible beginnings: (A) *demi-plié* in fifth position *croisé*, push from both feet upward and forward into the air, straightening the legs but keeping them closely together. Turn to the *effacé* direction as the back leg opens to *effacé derrière* and land on the front foot in *fondu*. Or, (B) following the push into the air, immediately open the back leg as the body turns to *effacé*. Land on the forward leg in *fondu*, with the back leg remaining extended *effacé derrière*. Completion of the step also has alternative versions: (A) pass

FAILLI

the back foot forward through first position *demi-plié* to fourth position with the weight distributed equally on both legs in *demi-plié*. Or, (B) after passing through to fourth position, transfer the weight well forward over the front leg in *fondu* as the back leg extends.

Note The differences above may be dictated by stylistic preference, by the nature of the step to follow the preparatory *failli*, and/or by the dynamics and speed of the music. In any case, the timing of the *failli* is like that of the *demi-contretemps*— the initial spring into the air is on the upbeat, with the entire step completed in one count. Thus, the meaning of the term *failler*, to give way or yield, is reflected in both the design and the timing of the step.

The movement of the arms in *failli* contrasts with that used in *demi-contretemps*, where usually a *bras bas* position is held throughout. Here, the arms open swiftly to the side in a *demi-seconde* or higher position as the leg opens to *effacé* in the air. Upon landing, the arms usually assume a position of preparation for the next step.

CONTRETEMPS (kohn-treh-TAHn)

This term, literally meaning "against time," actually means several different things according to different stylistic schools. Two possibilities are offered here.

Description Begin either in fifth position right foot front, or with the left foot *pointe tendue derrière*, body *en croisé*. (A) Execute a *coupé dessus*: make a small *rond de jambe en dedans* with the left leg as the right lowers *en fondu*, and, with or without a spring into the air, quickly transfer the weight to the left foot *en fondu*, right foot *sur le cou-de-pied*, body turned slightly to the right. Immediately step out onto the right foot, either to *demi-pointe* or *fondu*, depending upon the movement to follow. This sequence also may be done *en face*, with the last step *en avant* or *à la seconde*.

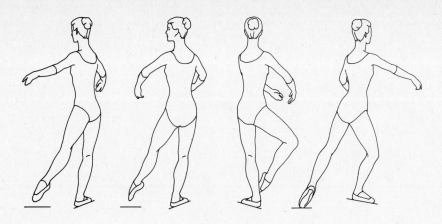

CONTRETEMPS

Or, (B) following the *coupé dessus*, immediately slide the right leg to fourth position *devant en effacé*, and quickly close the left foot to *demi-plié* fifth position behind, body *en effacé*. Complete this version with a *demi-contretemps* as described above, but without change of body direction.

Note Open the arms *à la seconde* in the preparatory pose. During the *coupé dessus*, quickly close the arms *en avant* or *demi-avant*. In version A they then will open outward in anticipation of the succeeding movement. In version B they will remain in position for the *demi-contretemps*.

SISSONNE TOMBÉE (see-SON tohn-BAY)

Another connecting step, this one is essentially a *sissonne simple* followed by a *tombé*. It may be done forward (usually to *croisé* or *effacé* directions), to the side, or even backward.

Description To perform *en avant* to the *effacé* direction, *demi-plié* in fifth position right foot front. Push off both feet straight into the air, raising the front foot *sur le cou-de-pied devant* (just above the ankle of the back leg), and land in *fondu* on the left leg. (This completes the *sissonne simple*.) Immediately open the right leg forward in the *effacé* direction, then fall forward in *fondu* on it, extending the left leg to *effacé derrière à terre* or slightly off the ground. (This completes the *tombé*.)

Note The step may be done with a high jump, in which case the front foot is raised to the *retiré* position (just below the knee) during the *sissonne simple*. The *tombé* often is followed by a *pas de bourrée*, which is a convenient connecting step between the *sissonne tombée* and perhaps a following jump or *pirouette*.

An alternate, but similar version, calls for a slide forward, rather than a *tombé*. Usually this version is called *temps levé chassé*.

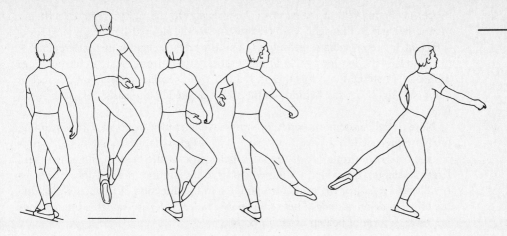

SISSONNE TOMBÉE

ASSEMBLÉ PORTÉ (ah-sahn-BLAY por-TAY)

The different qualities of this traveling *assemblé* are indicated by its alternate titles: *assemblé élancé* (darting) or *assemblé de volée* (flying). Unlike the usual *assemblé en place,* where the weight of the body remains entirely over the supporting leg while the other leg extends outward in preparation for the jump, the traveling *assemblé* requires the body, and particularly the head, anticipate the new direction even as the preparation for the jump is being made.

Description To perform *assemblé porté derrière, demi-plié* in fifth position right foot back, then *dégagé* the right foot along the floor to the side as the left knee bends

ASSEMBLÉ PORTÉ

deeper in *fondu*. With a strong push upwards and to the right, spring into the air off the left leg as the right leg lifts smoothly to the desired height (45 degrees is sufficient for intermediate technique). The torso leans slightly in the direction of flight, so that the left leg can be brought quickly up in front of the right, both legs momentarily straight and together in the air. Land simultaneously on both feet in *demi-plié*, right foot still behind, on the spot indicated by the earlier lift of the right foot.

Note   Higher *assemblés portés*, or those traveling forward or backward or turning, often are preceded by a preparatory step, such as *glissade*, *pas de basque*, or *pas de bourrée couru*. A strong lift of the arms helps sustain the pose in the air in these larger *assemblés*, but when performed closer to the ground, more *élancé*, the arms usually are *en bas*, or the arm corresponding to the direction of travel is *en bas* and the other *en demi-seconde*. These smaller *assemblés portés* are valuable preparations for *brisés*, a form of beaten *assemblé porté*.

EMBOITÉ (ahn-bwah-TAY)

This spring from one foot to the other (being thus a form of *jeté*, but without a brush on the floor) brings the raised leg to a low *attitude* position directly in front (for *emboité devant*) or in back (for *emboité derrière*) of the supporting leg.

Description   To begin a series of *emboités devant* from fifth position right foot back, *demi-plié* and push from both feet into the air, bringing the right foot forward to a low *attitude* position *devant*. Land in *fondu* on the left foot. From the *fondu*, push into the air, bringing the left foot forward to the *attitude* position, and land in *fondu* on the right foot. Continue in this manner, springing from one foot to the other. *Emboités* may be done *sur place* or traveling forward or backward. (See section of turning steps for *emboités en tournant*.)

Emboités sur les pointes (sewr lay PWAHnT) are done on half- or full-point without the spring into the air. From fifth position, the back leg opens slightly to the side with straight knee and pointed toes, then closes to fifth position front on half- or full-point. The series continues, alternating legs, without lowering the heels or bending the knees. The same movement may be reversed, closing to fifth position back each time.

Note   The step derives its name from the verb, *emboiter*, to fit in or encase. Thus, whether done *sur les pointes* or *en l'air*, each leg must appear to create a frame around the other.

PAS DE CHEVAL (pah duh shuh-VAHL)

Description   Beginning from *pointe tendue devant*, *fondu* on the supporting leg and brush the pointed foot inward to the supporting knee. *Développé devant à la demi-hauteur* and lower again to *pointe tendue*. The brush and *développé* may occur with a *relevé* or a *temps levé*.

PASSE-PIED (pahss-pee-AY)

As the name implies, *passe-pied* is a passing of the feet, which may be forward, backward, or sideward. Performed with a slight spring, it is a form of *jeté*, but usually performed on half- or full-point.

Description   *Demi-plié* and push slightly into the air while extending or developing the front leg to any given direction. Alight in *fondu* on the other leg as the extending leg touches the ground at *pointe tendue*. Continue by springing off the supporting foot and then extending it to the given direction while landing on the other foot.

Note   *Passe-pied* does not require a brush inward, as in *pas de cheval*, but is satisfied with merely a switch of feet. It is especially fun to do in a 6/8 rhythm.

MORE *SISSONNES*

This versatile step has thirty-nine listings in one contemporary dictionary.[3] Here, a few varieties are chosen for the intermediate level. The characteristic *sissonne* movement, a jump from two feet to one foot, is to be found somewhere within each of these variations.

SISSONNE CHANGÉE (see-SON shahn-ZHAY)

Traveling either forward or backward, this *sissonne* has a change of feet in the air before landing.

Description   To perform *en avant* (traveling forward), *demi-plié* in fifth position right foot front, push from both feet into the air and forward with straight legs. Immediately switch the legs so that the left comes forward. Land on the left foot in *fondu*, the right leg extended backward. Quickly slide the right foot to fifth position

**MEDIUM-SIZE
ALLEGRO STEPS**

SISSONNE CHANGÉE EN AVANT

back in *demi-plié*. For *sissonne changée en arrière* (traveling backward), the foot that was front switches to the back and alights in *fondu*.

Note *Sissonnes* that travel sideward with a change of feet usually are called simply *sissonne dessus* (if the back foot opens to the side and finishes front) or *sissonne dessous* (if the front foot opens to the side and finishes back). Any traveling *sissonne* requires that the head and the spine anticipate the new direction while the body is in the air, thus already establishing the pose that will be seen upon landing.

SISSONNE PASSÉE (see-SON pah-SAY)

Here the action resembles *relevé passé*, but with a spring into the air replacing the *relevé*.

Description For *sissonne passée dessous*, *demi-plié* in fifth position right foot front, push off both feet straight upward into the air. Immediately raise the right foot sharply to the side of the left knee. Land in *fondu* on the left foot, and quickly lower the right foot to fifth position back in *demi-plié*. Reverse the action for *sissonne passée dessus* by bringing the back foot up to the knee and closing front at the finish of the step. The direction of the movement is upward, not traveling in any other direction.

SISSONNE PASSÉE

SISSONNE RETOMBÉE (see-SON ruh-tohn-BAY)

This is a compound step, that is, it includes more than one step. It begins with a *sissonne ouverte de coté*, followed immediately by a *coupé* and an *assemblé*. The *sissonne retombée* may be done in a series traveling across the room, or it may alternate sides.

Description To execute one form of *sissonne retombée dessous, demi-plié* in fifth position left foot front. Push from both feet and spring into the air, traveling to the right while opening the left leg to the side, either with a *battement* or *développé*. Land in *fondu* on the right foot, and immediately *coupé dessous* with the left leg, raising the right foot *sur le cou-de-pied devant*, and then *assemblé dessous* with the right leg. The step now may be repeated to the same direction. In order to alternate sides, the *sissonne de coté* is taken in the direction of the front foot each time.

SISSONNE RETOMBÉE

Note This step has a gentle falling quality from side to side, hence its name—*retombée*—to fall again. The body inclines in the direction the *sissonne* travels, then straightens on the *coupé* only to incline again, but slightly away from the direction of the *assemblé*. Given this quality, the term *sissonne retombée* is more descriptive of the step than the alternative name, *sissonne doublée*.

The timing for the sequence usually is: *sissonne* (count *one*), *coupé* (count *and*), *assemblé* (count *two*). See Chapter 5, p. 113, for suggestions of *port de bras* to help sustain the body in the air.

TEMPS DE CUISSE (tahn duh KWEES)

This form of *sissonne* is preceded by either a *battement dégagé* or a *battement retiré*, either of which closes quickly to fifth position *demi-plié* in preparation for the *sissonne*. If the *retiré* preparation is used, it is with the foot only slightly lifted from the floor, not raised to the knee. Even so, this preparation, with the slight lift of the thigh, seems to follow more closely the meaning of the term, *cuisse* being the French word for thigh. *Temps de cuisse* usually travels from side to side, but it may also move forward or backward.

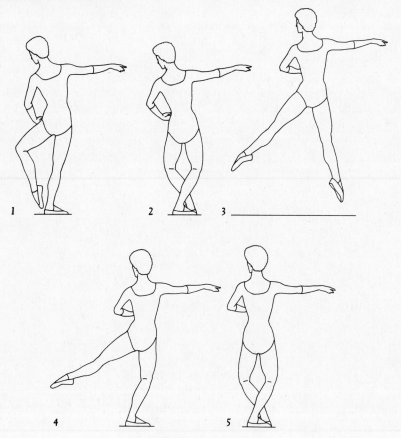

TEMPS DE CUISSE DESSUS

Description To perform *temps de cuisse dessus*, from fifth position right foot front, quickly *retiré* the left foot to the side of the supporting ankle (or *dégagé à la seconde*) and close to fifth position front in *demi-plié*. Push off both feet into the air, traveling to the right (toward the back foot). Land in *fondu* on the right foot and quickly slide the extended left foot into fifth position front *demi-plié*. The action is reversed for *temps de cuisse dessous*.

Note This is a perky step, with the quick preparation of *retiré* or *dégagé* being on count "*and*," then the small *sissonne* on count "*one*." A simple and effective position for the arms in *temps de cuisse dessus* is with the forward arm corresponding to the leg that is brought front. See Chapter 5, p. 113, for use of the head in the step.

BALLONNÉ (bah-loh-NAY)

MORE MEDIUM-SIZE STEPS

The bouncing quality of *ballonné* must be achieved by a push-off from only one foot while the other leg makes a *battement* in any given direction—to the front, side, or back.

Description To perform to the *effacé devant* direction, *dégagé* the right foot forward to *effacé* while making a *fondu* on the left leg. Without pause, lift the right leg to 45 degrees, as in a *battement devant*, and simultaneously push from the left foot into the air. For an instant both legs will be straight. Land in *fondu* on the left leg while lowering the right foot *sur le cou-de-pied devant*. From this position the step can be repeated. When done in a series, *ballonnés* often travel in the direction of the *battement*. The position of the arms, head, and body (in this example, the *effacé* position) must be established before the spring into the air and should be maintained while airborne and upon landing.

BALLONNÉ

Note As in most jumping steps, in *ballonné* the dancer is airborne on count *"and,"* then returns to the floor on count *"one."* The action and timing of *ballonné* can be practiced in a series of quick *battements fondus* with *relevés*, either at *barre* or in center floor: *battement* to the given direction while rising to *demi-pointe* on the supporting foot (count *and, fondu* on the supporting leg and bend the raised leg into *sur le cou-de-pied devant* or *derrière* (count *one*). These are strenuous movements, both as an exercise and in the step itself, demanding careful attention to the alignment of the knee and foot of the supporting leg in *fondu*.

BALLOTTÉ (bah-loh-TAY)

Ballotter literally means "to toss about," suggesting the lightness required in the step, which in essence consists of *coupés dessous* and *dessus*. When performed well, *ballottés* convey an image of the body rocking easily backward and forward in the air as the weight changes. The apparent ease is deceptive, however, because the step requires a great deal of strength, control, and careful timing. *Ballottés* usually are performed in a series in *effacé* and may be done with straight legs or with *retirés*.

Description To perform a *ballotté en avant* with straight knees, begin in *croisé* position, left foot *pointe tendue derrière*, arms *en bas*. *Fondu* on the right leg as the left leg raises slightly in the air, spring upward off the right foot and immediately

BALLOTTÉ EN AVANT ET EN ARRIÈRE

join the legs in fifth position *en l'air*, body turning to *effacé* and beginning to lean backward, arms *en avant*. Land in *fondu* on the left leg, body leaning slightly more backward, right leg extending forward, by means of a small *développé*, to 45 degrees in *effacé*, right arm opened *à la seconde*.

To perform the same type of *ballotté en arrière* (often following without pause the one *en avant*), spring upward off the left foot, and again, join the legs in fifth position *en l'air* and the arms *en avant*, body remaining in *effacé* but now beginning to lean forward. Land in *fondu* on the right leg, body leaning slightly more forward, the left leg extending backward, by means of a small *développé*, to 45 degrees in *effacé*, left arm opened *à la seconde*. (This version of *ballotté* may travel slightly forward and backward during the springs.)

To perform a *ballotté en avant* with *retirés*, begin as above, but, during the spring into the air, lift and bend the knees sharply so the toes are drawn together in fifth position, body turning to *effacé* and beginning to lean backward. Land in *fondu* on the left leg, body leaning slightly more backward as the right leg continues to develop forward to 90 degrees in *effacé*.

To perform this version of *ballotté en arrière*, spring upward off the left foot and again sharply lift and bend the knees, joining the feet together with the toes in fifth position *en l'air*, body remaining in *effacé* but beginning to lean forward. Land in *fondu* on the right leg, body leaning slightly more forward as the left leg continues to develop backward to 90 degrees in *effacé*. The arm movement is the same as in the previous version.

Note *Ballottés* done in a series, alternating *en avant* and *en arrière*, should occur without pausing in the *fondus*. However, the *fondus* must be particularly secure—heel firmly on the ground, knee well bent and in careful alignment with the supporting foot—in order to maximize the spring into the air (and to minimize strain on the body). The torso should be controlled so the chest remains well lifted during the forward and backward motions. The height of the jump and of the extended or developed leg will depend upon the speed of the music and the other steps that follow in the combination. (The quicker the music, the lower the jump and the extensions. If larger steps, such as *tour jeté*, follow *ballottés*, then *ballotté* extensions and elevation will be lower in order not to detract from the more important step.)

PAS DE PAPILLON (pah duh pa-pee-YOHN)
or *JETÉ PASSÉ* (zhuh-TAY pah-SAY)
This "step of the butterfly," or passing *jeté*, is delightful both to watch and to perform. It can travel forward or backward, but always should have a delicate lightness to the spring from one leg to the other—a most effective sight when a series of these *jetés* are performed across the room.

Description To perform *en avant*, the most common direction, begin in *croisé* position right foot *pointe tendue derrière*. *Glissé* (glide) forward with the right foot through first position to fourth position *effacé*, allowing the weight to transfer to the right leg in a deep *fondu* as the left leg is raised backward in *attitude* or *arabesque*. Push from the right leg into the air and raise the right leg backward past the left into a higher *attitude* or *arabesque*. For an instant both legs are raised in the air behind the body. Land in *fondu* on the left leg, with the right leg in *attitude croisée* behind.

PAS DE PAPILLON

Note   A slight torso movement and a flowing *port de bras* add to the beauty of this step: allow the torso to tilt slightly forward during the *glissé* into *effacé* on the right foot (in some styles, the torso also is allowed to lean slightly to the right at this moment); during the spring, straighten the torso and lift the right arm upward from the side (the visual effect is almost that of bending back with the torso); upon landing, the pose must be *attitude croisé* with the right arm high and, in some styles, the torso leaning slightly to the left.

LARGE
***ALLEGRO* STEPS**

GRAND JETÉ (grahn zhuh-TAY)

This large leap usually is done forward (*en avant*) following a preparatory step of some kind, such as *chassé, pas de bourreé couru,* or *sissonne tombée.* The nineteenth-century romantic style requires an upward, arching jump, whereas the contemporary form is more horizontal and darting. Both must begin from a strong *fondu* on the front leg that then will help propel the body both upward and forward into the air as the other leg brushes forward in a *grand battement.*

Description   For the romantic style of high arching *grand jeté,* make a *fondu* on the forward leg and allow the torso to stretch upward and slightly backward as the back leg brushes forward in a high *battement.* This helps direct the upward curve of the *grand jeté* during the strong push-off from the *fondu.* As the descent from the *jeté* begins, an *arabesque* pose is already established in the air. The weight then falls well forward over the front leg as it lands in a deep *fondu,* the other leg still extended backward in *arabesque.*

For the contemporary horizontal, almost splitting *grand jeté,* take a *fondu* on the forward leg, allowing the torso to reach slightly forward. Push off from that supporting leg as, almost simultaneously, a rapid *battement en avant* is made with the other leg. The effect is of two legs stretching outward at almost the same time, one cutting forward and the other backward. The torso remains as quiet as possible during the rapid extension of the legs.

Note Not only must the leading foot point strongly and quickly to direct the body forward and upward, but, upon landing, it must release sufficiently to allow a deep *fondu* of the supporting knee. By contrast, the other foot, having pushed off strongly from the floor to propel the body forward and upward, must retain its sharp point during the descent and landing.

As a general rule, alignment of the shoulders with the rest of the torso is easier to maintain in second than in first *arabesque*. Therefore, *grands jetés* done with opposition—for example, if the right leg executes the *battement en avant*, bring the left arm forward—are the most effective for first attempts. This is true for the following exercise.

TEMPS LEVÉ EN ARABESQUE (tahn luh-VAY ah na-ra-BESK)

A *temps levé* is a hop from one foot followed by a landing on the same foot. The other leg may be raised to any desired position, but in this example it is extended behind in *arabesque*. *Arabesque sautée* is another term for this step.

Description To perform in second *arabesque*, stand with the weight well centered over the right leg, the left leg extended straight behind at the desired height and the left arm extended forward. Without otherwise altering the pose, *fondu* on the right leg and push from the right foot into the air, quickly pointing the foot and completely extending the leg. Land on the right foot in *fondu*, maintaining the pose in second *arabesque*.

Note This step is used in a variety of ways: as a preparatory movement before other steps in a combination (for example, *temps levé en arabesque, pas de bourrée couru en arrière*, and *assemblé en tournant*); as an exiting step after a combination performed across the room (perhaps the above combination, plus three *piqués tours en dedans*, finishing with a *temps levé en arabesque*); as a series of *temps levés*, done with one or more simple running steps in between. All these examples of *temps levés* may be done quickly and with only slight elevation, or they may be done slower and higher, depending upon the phrasing and speed of the music. In the latter case, a slight wrist and elbow movement can enhance the lift from the floor: during the *fondu* preparation, press very slightly downward with the wrists and elbows, then, during the push from the floor, raise them to their original position. No other change in the position of the body should occur before, during, or after the *temps levé* other than this very subtle wrist and elbow action, along with the stretching of the supporting leg.

TURNING STEPS

Most *allegro* steps also can be performed as turning steps, in which case the words *en tournant* usually are added to the name (e.g., *chassé en tournant*). Other *allegro* steps *always* involve a turn, but their names may or may not reflect this movement (e.g., *tour en l'air, saut de basque*). Many turning *allegro* steps can be appropriately introduced to the intermediate student.

BALANCÉ EN TOURNANT (bah-lah*n*-SAY ahn toor-NAHN)

The relatively simple, but lovely, *balancé* may be done with a half-turn or a whole turn, usually to a waltz rhythm.

Description   To perform with half-turns moving sideward, from fifth position right foot back, body *en face, demi-plié* and *dégagé* the right foot to the side. Spring from *fondu* on the left leg, and land in *fondu* on the right leg as the body makes one quarter-turn to the right. Step onto the left *demi-pointe* directly behind the right foot, turning the body one quarter-turn to the right as the right foot releases the ground. Lower the right foot in *fondu*, and raise the left foot directly behind the supporting ankle (*sur le cou-de-pied derrière*). The front of the body now faces up-

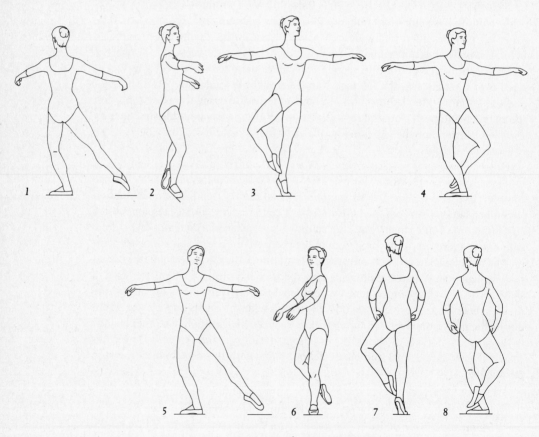

BALANCÉ EN TOURNANT

stage. To perform the second *balancé* half-turn, *dégagé* the left leg to the side. Spring from *fondu* on the right leg to *fondu* on the left as the body makes one quarter-turn to the right. Quickly bring the right foot behind the left and step onto the right *demi-pointe*, turning the body one quarter-turn to the right as the left foot releases the ground. Lower the left foot in *fondu*, and raise the right foot *sur le cou-de-pied derrière*. The front of the body faces downstage once again.

Balancés en tournant also can be performed with a forward *dégagé* and spring to begin the first half-turn, and a backward *dégagé* and spring to begin the second half-turn.

A complete turn of only one *balancé* usually turns to the opposite direction from that of the first step, thus adding an element of surprise to an *enchaînement*. For example, if the first spring is made to the right, the body will turn to the left before the landing in *fondu*, and it will continue to turn left during the step onto *demi-pointe* and the final step in *fondu*.

Note A variety of *port de bras* can be used for these traveling turns. The simplest, perhaps, is an opening of the arms through *en avant* to second position during the first *balancé* half-turn, and a lowering of the arms *en bas* during the second half-turn.

PAS DE BOURRÉE EN TOURNANT (pah duh boo-RAY aan toor-NAHN)

A complete turn, either *en dedans* or *en dehors*, can be made with the three steps of a *pas de bourrée*. If *en dedans*, the turn is made inward toward the supporting leg after the preparatory movement, usually a *battement dégagé à la seconde*. If *en dehors*, the turn is made outward toward the leg that makes the preparatory movement.

Description For *pas de bourrée en dedans* (essentially a turning *bourrée dessus*, because the direction of the three steps is front, side, back), *demi-plié* in fifth position right foot front, and, remaining in *fondu* on the right leg, *dégagé* the left foot to second position just a few inches above the ground. Close the left foot to fifth position front, stepping onto it on *demi-pointe*, and make a half-turn to the right, releasing the right foot. Step onto the right *demi-pointe*, and make another half-turn to the right, releasing the left foot. Close the left foot behind to fifth position *demi-plié*. Depending on the step to follow, the turn may instead finish in *fondu* on the back foot, with the front foot arched just above the supporting ankle.

For *pas de bourrée en dehors* (essentially a turning *bourrée dessous*, because the direction of the three steps is back, side, front), *demi-plié*, and, remaining in *fondu* on the left leg, *dégagé* the right foot to second position just a few inches above the ground. Close the right foot to fifth position back by stepping onto it on *demi-pointe*, and turn half-way around to the right, releasing the left foot. Step onto the left *demi-pointe*, and make another half-turn to the right, releasing the right foot. Close the right foot front in fifth position *demi-plié*, or lower to *fondu* and arch the left foot behind the supporting ankle.

Note During the preparatory *dégagé*, the arms usually open to *demi-seconde* and then close to *demi-avant* for the turn. The head focuses front as long as possible before rapidly turning in the direction of the *pas de bourrée*. The coordination and timing of the head and arm movements is critical whether the step is used as a preparatory movement, a connecting movement, or in a series of alternating *pas de bourrées en dedans* and *en dehors*.

EN DEDANS

EN DEHORS

PAS DE BOURRÉE EN TOURNANT

To enhance the momentum of the turns, the preparatory *dégagé* may have a slight circular route, rather than extending directly *à la seconde*. The entire step can be executed in one count ("*and a one*"), but it can be learned first to a slower count ("*and one and two*").

ASSEMBLÉ EN TOURNANT (ah-sahn-BLAY ahn toor-NAHN)

Description The momentum for this turning jump often comes from a preparatory step, such as *pas de bourrée couru en arrière*. Following the *bourrée*, which has turned the body to face upstage, brush the back leg forward through first position *demi-plié* and make a *grand battement devant* as the supporting leg pushes into the air. Turn *en dedans* in the air to face the front of the room, closing the *battement* to fifth position front *en l'air*, then land in *demi-plié*.

Note A more accurate appellation for this step would be *assemblé dessus en dedans*, because it is performed in that direction. The half-turn of the body during the preceding *bourrée* means that the *assemblé en tournant* is only a half-turn itself. In more advanced technique, it can be increased to a turn-and-a-half, the legs joining immediately to fifth position *en l'air*.

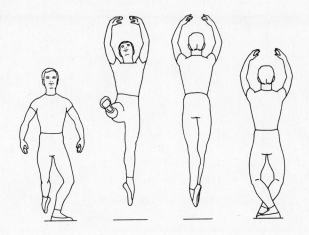

ASSEMBLÉ EN TOURNANT

Although the impetus for the jump comes from the action of the legs, it is enhanced by the placement of the weight well forward in the preparatory *fondu* (the final movement of the *bourrée*), and by the swift action of the arms. They should open outward during the *bourrée*, lowering quickly to *bras bas* during the last step in *fondu*, then rise directly *en haut* during the *assemblé en tournant*.

EMBOÎTÉ EN TOURNANT (ahn-bwah-TAY ahn toor-NAHN)

Not so difficult as most *jetés en tournant*, the turning *emboîté* is a perky addition to the dancer's *allegro* vocabulary. A complete turn consists of two *emboîtés devant*, often performed in a series across the room.

Description To travel to the right, from fifth position right foot front, *demi-plié*, and spring upward and to the right from both feet, bringing the back foot

STEPS OF ELEVATION THAT ALSO TURN

forward into a low *attitude devant* as the body makes a half-turn to the right in the air. Land in *fondu* on the right leg, the front of the body facing upstage. From the *fondu*, immediately spring upward into the air, making another half-turn to the right as the right leg is brought forward into a low *attitude*. Land in *fondu* on the left foot, the body facing downstage once more. For a series, continue in this manner, springing from one foot to the other and traveling toward stage right with each half-turn. The raised foot may be placed *sur le cou-de-pied devant*, rather than in *attitude devant*.

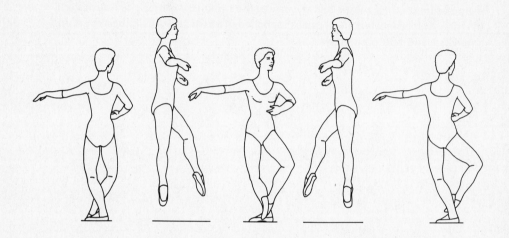

EMBOÎTÉ EN TOURNANT

Note The spotting of the head and the coordination of the arms assist the brisk execution of *emboîtés en tournant*. When preparing from *plié* or *fondu*, the forward arm corresponds to the forward leg, the other arm being *à la seconde*. During each spring into the air, the forward arm opens quickly to the side and remains there as the other arm closes from second to *avant*. The focus is toward the direction of travel. Thus, the head will turn toward the left shoulder after the first half-turn to the right, then snap quickly around to the right shoulder during the second half-turn.

CHASSÉ EN TOURNANT (shah-SAY ahn toor-NAHN)

This is a compound step that has many forms. It may begin either with a *coupé dessous en tournant* or a *tour en l'air* followed by a *chassé en avant*. Both of these versions usually are found in more advanced technique, but there is yet another type to consider here. It is described with a simple preparatory *chassé* preceding each turning *chassé*.

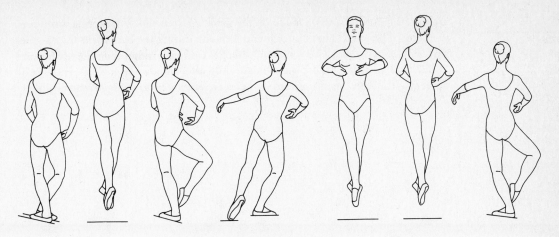

CHASSÉ EN TOURNANT

Description Face the *effacé* direction, right foot front in fifth position. *Demi-plié* and spring into the air. Land in *fondu* on the back foot with the right foot arched just above the supporting ankle *(sur le cou-de-pied devant)*. Immediately lower the right foot and slide it forward to fourth position, transferring the weight to the right leg in *fondu*. Spring into the air, immediately closing the left leg behind the right in fifth position *en l'air*, and make a complete turn to the right. Land in *fondu* on the left leg with the right foot *sur le cou-de-pied devant*, and slide forward again to fourth position. Spring into the air, closing the left leg behind the right *en l'air*, and land in *fondu* on the back foot. Continue in this manner, alternating a simple *chassé* with a turning *chassé*. Later a series of only *chassés en tournant* can be attempted.

Note During the preparatory *chassé*, the forward arm corresponds to the forward leg, the other arm being *à la seconde*. During the turn in the air, the open arm closes to the other so that the turn is made with both arms *en avant* or *demi-avant*. The same arm opens again to the side upon landing in *fondu*. As in any traveling turn, the head must focus toward the direction traveled, and the weight of the body must be well forward over the supporting leg.

FOUETTÉ SAUTÉ EN TOURNANT

(fweh-TAY soh-TAY ahn toor-NAHN)

Description The fundamental movements of this step already have been described in Chapter 3 (see *fouetté en relevé*, pp. 61–63). The difference here is the *temps levé*, or spring into the air, instead of the *relevé* during the *grand battement devant*. As soon as the pose is established at the full height of the *battement* and the *temps levé*, the body makes a quick half-turn, rotating the leg in its hip socket to *arabesque*, before landing in *fondu* on the same leg from which the spring was taken.

Note The arms help control the movement: during the *battement* they ascend forcefully moving past *avant* to *haut* (directly overhead, rather than slightly forward of the head as usual), where they remain until after the turn in the air. As the body descends, the arms open outward, either *à la seconde* or to an *arabesque* position.

FOUETTÉ SAUTÉ EN TOURNANT

Although often preceded by a traveling step, such as *pas de bourrée couru en arrière*, the *fouetté* itself is done in place (*sur place*). It is a step of high elevation, used in grand *allegro* combinations where it is often called simply *grand fouetté*. A more advanced form involving a *complete* turn in the air is, therefore, more aptly termed *grand fouetté en tournant*.

TOUR JETÉ (toor zhuh-TAY)

Although *tour jeté* is not the correct name, it is used more frequently than the step's proper titles: *grand jeté entrelacé* or *grand jeté dessus en tournant*. The preferred common usage will be observed here.

Description From *pointe tendue derrière* with the right foot, *fondu* on the supporting leg and raise the back leg to 45 degrees. With a strong push from the *fondu*, turn toward the extended right leg and step onto it, lowering through the ball of the foot to *fondu*. Brush the left foot through first position *demi-plié*, and thrust it forward, as though making a *grand battement devant*, while the supporting leg pushes forcefully from the floor. Quickly make a half-turn to the right *en l'air* as the legs, fully stretched, closely pass one another. Land in *fondu* on the left leg, with the right leg extended to *arabesque*.

Note In the preparatory *fondu* before the *tour jeté*, the arms open strongly to second position so that they can lower sharply *en bas* as the leg passes through first position *demi-plié*. The arms then quickly ascend in front of the body and directly overhead *en haut* during the *grand battement* and second half-turn. This helps establish the strong lift of the spine necessary for control of the step. During the descent to *arabesque fondu*, the arms open quickly outward to the desired pose.

Even though the jump and turn in the air occur in one place, greater momentum for the *tour jeté* comes from a preceding traveling movement, such as a *glissade* and a step outward, or, stronger yet, a *pas de bourrée couru*. The close passing, or

TOUR JETÉ

interlacing effect of the legs in the air is the distinctive feature of the *tour jeté*, and thus must be accomplished by very straight forward and backward *battements*, not by *ronds de jambe* movements with relaxed knees.

SAUT DE BASQUE (soh duh BAHSK)

In this step the dancer travels through space, making a complete turn in the air with one foot drawn up to *retiré* position. Although it may be performed only slightly above the ground, *saut de basque* is most spectacular when performed with high elevation.

Description   To begin one version of *saut de basque* turning to the right, *fondu* on the left leg, and either *dégagé* to the side or *retiré* with the right foot. Step out onto the right foot in *fondu*, push from that foot into the air, and make a half-turn traveling to the side while thrusting the left leg *à la seconde*. Continue turning to the right to face front again, landing in *fondu* on the left leg, with the right foot raised sharply to the knee in the *retiré* position.

SAUT DE BASQUE

Note   The accompanying *port de bras* can be varied somewhat, but usually involves a strong opening of the arms to the side during the first half-turn and a closing *en avant* or *en haut* during the second half-turn.

Alternative versions of the step include: extension of both legs to the side during the first half-turn, or two sequential *retirés* before landing, the first by the leg that executed the leading *battement*. This latter form has a quality of *pas de chat*, because for an instant in the air both knees are sharply bent with the toes close together.

TOUR EN L'AIR (toor ahn lair)

The usual form of this step is simply a *changement en tournant*, a jump changing feet while making a complete turn in the air. A double *tour en l'air* is a standard technical expectation for advanced male dancers.

Description   For a *tour* to the right, *demi-plié* deeply in fifth position right foot front. Push from both feet into the air, straightening the legs and sharply pointing the feet. Make a complete turn to the right changing feet before landing in *demi-plié* left foot front.

Note   During the preparatory *plié*, the arms rise, the forward arm corresponding to the front leg, the other arm *à la seconde*. As the jump and turn are made, the open arm closes forcefully inward to join the front arm, giving impetus to the turn without changing the alignment of the shoulders over the hips. Additional impetus is given by the quick spotting of the head, which actually leads the body around. There is no momentary lingering focus to the front, as in *pirouettes*.

Preparatory exercises of quarter- and half-*tours* follow the same general rules and are valuable practices for achieving the strong verticality necessary for the complete *tour*.

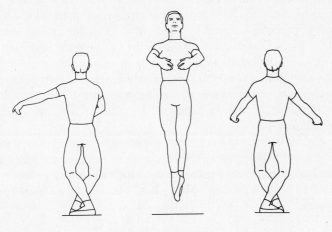

TOUR EN L'AIR

STEPS WITH BEATS

Collectively known as *batterie* (bat-REE), steps with beats are categorized according to their requirements for elevation, the *grande batterie* (such as *cabriole*) utilizing high elevation, or the *petite batterie* (such as *entrechats*) needing relatively little elevation. Further divisions are made for those steps where one leg beats against the other (*cabrioles*) or where both legs beat with equal vigor (*entrechats*). When an ordinary step is embellished with a beat the term *battu* is added to its name (*assemblé battu*).

SAUTÉ EN SECONDE BATTU (soh-TAY ahn suh-GOHnD bah-TEW)

This is one of the best preparations for *batterie*, being a series of jumps in second position taken with a beat of the legs before each landing.

Description   To prepare for *grande batterie*, *demi-plié* in second position and push high into the air, fully stretching the legs and arching the feet. At the height of the jump, and with the legs well turned out, beat the calves together, right leg in front. Open both legs and land in second position *demi-plié*. Repeat, beating with the left leg front. Continue for a series of *sautés*, alternating beats in this manner.

To prepare for rapid *petite batterie*, *demi-plié* in a smaller second position and spring slightly off the ground, extending the legs and sharply arching the feet, but not necessarily completely straightening the knees. Immediately bring the legs together, crossing the right foot well in front so that both heels are visible as the legs beat from the base of the calves downwards. Open both legs and land in a small second position *demi-plié*. Continue in a series, alternating the leg that beats in front.

ÉCHAPPÉ SAUTÉ BATTU (ay-shah-PAY soh-TAY-bah-TEW)

Next in order of practice is *échappé battu*, done in its simplest form—a jump from fifth to second position, followed by a beat of the legs during the return jump to fifth position. Like *sauté battu*, the *échappé battu* may be performed relatively slowly with high elevation, or rapidly with only slight elevation.

Description   *Demi-plié* in fifth position right foot front, and spring into the air. Land in second position *demi-plié* and spring again into the air, bringing the legs together with the right leg front. Open the legs slightly and land in fifth position *demi-plié* right foot back.

Note   The leg that was in front before the *échappé* is the one that is front during the beat and then finishes in back. The step thus can continue in a series, alternating sides. Beats beginning from an open position, such as second, generally are easier to perform than beats beginning from a closed position, which therefore follow in order of practice.

ROYALE (rawh-YAL)

Actually a change of feet with a beat, *royale* is the common name for *changement battu*. It is performed rapidly with only slight elevation.

Description   *Demi-plié* in fifth position right foot front, and spring into the air, opening the legs slightly to the side. Bring the calves of the legs together, right leg front, open again to the side, and land in fifth position *demi-plié* right foot back.

Note   In a simple *royale*, such as this, the feet always change position after the beat. For all beats beginning from a closed position, the legs should open slightly before *and* after the beat in order to display the brilliancy of the action.

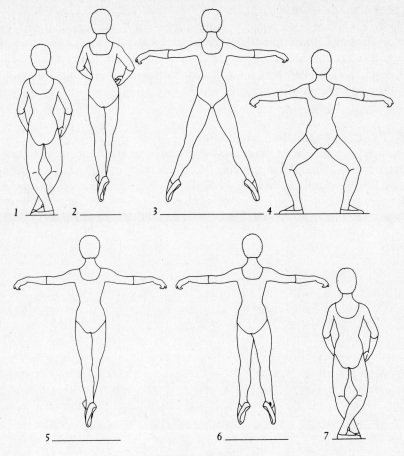

1   2 _____   3 _____   4

5 _____   6 _____   7

ÉCHAPPÉ SAUTÉ BATTU

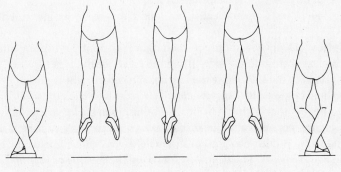

ROYALE

ENTRECHATS
(ahn-truh-SHAH)

The many varieties of *entrechat* reflect the Italian verb *intrecciare* (to braid or interlace), for all are small jumps with rapid crossings of the legs. *Entrechat* terminology describes the number of these crossings. Because both legs work with equal vigor, both are counted. Therefore, each crossing is considered as two movements, one by each leg. (An alternative way to determine the *entrechat* number is to count every opening and every closing of the legs.)

ENTRECHAT QUATRE (ahn-truh-shah KAH-truh)

The legs open, beat, open, and close—thus four (*quatre*) movements in this step.

Description   *Demi-plié* in fifth position right foot front and spring into the air, opening the legs slightly to the side. Bring the calves of the legs together, right leg back, open again to the side, and land in fifth position *demi-plié* right foot front.

Note   The foot that begins in front always finishes in front in *entrechat quatre*.

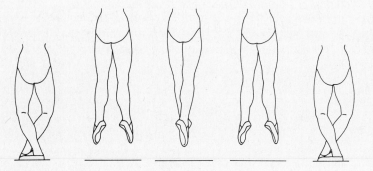

ENTRECHAT QUATRE

ENTRECHAT SIX (ahn-truh-shah SEES)

The legs open, beat, open, beat, open, and close—thus six movements in this step.

Description   *Demi-plié* in fifth position right foot front, and spring into the air, opening the legs slightly to the side. Bring the calves of the legs together, right leg back, open again to the side, bring the legs again together right leg front, open again to the side, and land in fifth position *demi-plié* right foot back.

Note   The foot that begins in front always finishes in back in *entrechat six*. More crossings require more elevation, and sometimes a preparatory step such as *soussus* (a springing *relevé* in fifth position) or *assemblé devant* adds impetus for bounding into the air for the beats. The *demi-plié* following the *soussus* or *assemblé* becomes the initiating or preparatory movement for *entrechat six*.

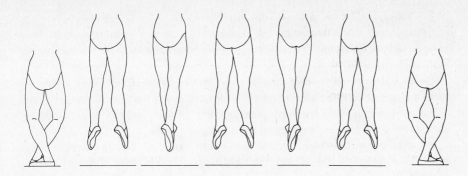

ENTRECHAT SIX

ENTRECHAT TROIS (ahn-truh-shah TRWAH)

Odd-numbered *entrechats (trois, cinq, sept*—three, five, seven*)* imply a landing on one foot, whereas even-numbered *entrechats (quatre, six, huit*—four, six, eight*)* always require a landing on both feet. *Entrechat trois* finishes on one foot with the other raised *sur le cou-de-pied,* either *devant* or *derrière.*

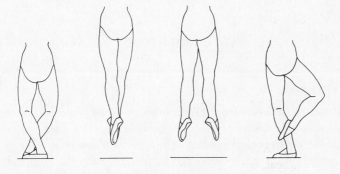

ENTRECHAT TROIS

Description For *entrechat trois derrière, demi-plié* in fifth position right foot front and spring into the air. The legs may be brought together immediately, or opened very slightly before beating, right leg front. Open the legs slightly to the side and land on the left leg in *fondu,* the right foot arched behind the supporting ankle.

For *entrechat trois devant,* begin with the right foot back, beat (right leg behind), and land in *fondu* on the left leg with the right foot arched in front of the supporting ankle.

ENTRECHAT CINQ (ahn-truh-shah SANK)

Several versions of this step give it considerable variety. The most common form in intermediate technique is similar to an *entrechat quatre* but with a finish on one foot, as in *entrechat trois*.

Description   For *entrechat cinq derrière*, *demi-plié* in fifth position right foot back, and spring into the air, opening the legs slightly to the side. Bring the calves of the legs together, right leg front, open again to the side, and land in *fondu* on the left leg, the right foot arched behind the supporting ankle.

For *entrechat cinq devant*, begin with the right foot front, beat (right leg behind), and land in *fondu* on the left leg, the right foot arched in front of the supporting ankle.

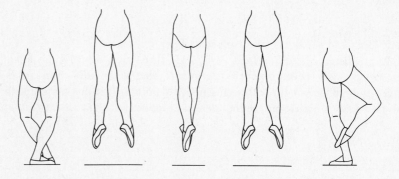

ENTRECHAT CINQ

More challenging versions include:

1. *Entrechat cinq fermé*, which begins from *demi-plié* in second position. During the spring into the air the legs are brought together, then beaten, as in an *entrechat quatre*, before landing in fifth position *demi-plié*.
2. *Entrechat cinq ouvert*, which begins from *demi-plié* in fifth position but finishes in second position after an *entrechat quatre* before landing.

Note   All *entrechats* benefit from preliminary practice of clean, rapid *battements dégagés à la seconde*. These can be performed in the same rhythm as the beating of any particular *entrechat*. For instance, a good practice for *entrechat quatre* would be a series of two quick *dégagés*, the first closing behind (count *and*) and the second closing in front (count *one*). This same exercise can be practiced on *demi-pointe*, with or without a lowering to *demi-plié* after the second *dégagé*. When the beat is combined with the jump, it first can be practiced facing the barre, so that the support of the arms can sustain the body longer in the air. However, it must be remembered that the rapidity of the crossings of the legs gives *entrechats* their brilliancy.

Unlike the preceding *batterie*, which are vertical jumps in place, *brisés* travel, usually diagonally forward or backward or to the side. For this reason, the incline of the body and the coordination of the arms play especially important roles. Simple *brisés* essentially are traveling *assemblés* with beats. They are considered *petite batterie*, performed rapidly with slight elevation.

BRISÉ DESSUS (bree-ZAY duh-SUI)

Description   *Demi-plié* in fifth position right foot back, and brush that foot slightly forward of second position, as in a *battement dégagé*. Push from the left leg into the air, traveling in the direction of the extended right leg. Bring the left leg to meet the right, beating the calves together, right leg front. Open the legs slightly and land in fifth position *demi-plié*, right foot back.

BRISÉ DESSUS

Note   During the action of the *brisé*, from the *dégagé* onward, the body inclines slightly forward toward the direction of travel, which in this case is a shallow diagonal. The arms may be *en bas* or *en avant*, or the forward arm may correspond to the leg that begins the action and the other arm open *demi-seconde*.

A common fault to beware of is any extra movement by the foot that springs from the floor; all too often it is allowed to turn inward following the *dégagé* by the other leg. The position of the front foot must remain turned-out throughout the execution of the step. Following the landing in *demi-plié*, the front foot must retain its firm position on the floor so that no extraneous step is taken.

BRISÉ DESSOUS (bree-ZAY duh-SOO)

Less frequently used, this *brisé* is the reverse of the one just described.

Description *Demi-plié* in fifth position left foot front, and *dégagé* that foot slightly behind the second position. Push from the right leg into the air, traveling in the direction of the extended left leg. Beat the calves together, right leg front, and land in *demi-plié*, left foot front.

Note The body inclines very slightly backward toward the direction of travel. The arms may rise to third *arabesque* (Cecchetti), or open *à la seconde*, or the forward arm may correspond to the leg that begins the action and the other arm open *à la seconde*.

A helpful preparation for *brisés* is a series of *assemblés derrière* to one side, followed by a series of *assemblés devant* to the other. The beating action may be practiced at barre, first with just a *relevé* from the supporting leg, later with the spring into the air. All these preparations should include the proper incline of the body so that the weight never falls away from the direction of travel.

CABRIOLES
(kah-bree-OHL)

This brief discussion of steps with beats concludes with the most challenging of all, for *cabrioles* require strong turn-out of the legs and high elevation. One leg is thrust into the air, followed by the other leg, which beats against it, sending the first leg higher. The legs must be completely straight and the feet extremely pointed as the calves are beaten. In all *cabrioles*, it is the underneath, or second leg, that rises to join the already raised leg. The two most frequently used *cabrioles* are described below.

CABRIOLE DEVANT EN EFFACÉE
(kah-bree-OHL duh-VAHn ah-neh-fah-SAY)

Description Standing *en effacé*, *demi-plié* in fifth position right foot front, and brush the right leg forward into the air to 45 degrees. Spring forward from the left leg into the air, and, without lowering the right leg, beat the calf of the left leg under it, sending the right leg higher. Land in *fondu* on the left leg. The right leg may remain in *effacé* in the air (for *cabriole ouverte*) or may close to fifth position front in *demi-plié* (for *cabriole fermée*).

Note The highlight of any *cabriole* is at the end, after the beat that sends the front leg higher while the body is still airborne. Therefore, in *cabriole devant* the initial *dégagé* of the front leg must not be too high, so that more height can be achieved after the beat. If the *dégagé* is unrealistically high, it also can cause the body to bend forward as the beat is attempted, thus destroying the lovely open line of the *effacé* position, with the body leaning slightly backward.

For more impetus into the *cabriole*, a preparatory step, such as *failli*, is helpful.

After landing from the *failli* in *fondu*, the back leg is brushed forward through first position to *effacé* in the air, and the action of *cabriole* continues as described above. Any such preparation should be discreet, however, not to detract from the *cabriole* itself.

CABRIOLE DEVANT EN EFFACÉE

CABRIOLE DERRIÈRE EN EFFACÉE
(kah-bree-OHL deh-reeAIR ah-neh-fah-SAY)

Description   Standing *en effacé*, *demi-plié* in fifth position right foot front, and brush the left leg backward in the air to 45 degrees. Spring backward from the right leg into the air, and, without lowering the left leg, beat the calf of the right leg under it, sending the left leg higher. Land in *fondu* on the right leg. The left leg may remain in *arabesque* or may close to fifth position back in *demi-plié*.

Note   Two errors often haunt the correct execution of this *cabriole*: the underneath leg is allowed to bend as it approaches the raised leg (an unpleasant sight), or the raised leg is not sufficiently turned-out, so the beat is against the shinbone instead of the calf (an unpleasant sensation).

The body should lean forward, but with the spine strongly lifted, in order to establish the *arabesque* line both in the air and upon landing. The arms may be in first, second, or third *arabesque* (Cecchetti), or any other harmonious design.

A good preparatory step is *sissonne tombée*, in which case the *cabriole derrière* begins from an open position, the back leg being already extended to *effacé*.

CABRIOLE DERRIÈRE EN EFFACÉE

It is hoped that the relatively few *allegro* selections briefly described in this chapter have given the reader some understanding of the ballet intricacies made possible by "knowing how to bend and straighten the knees at the proper time." That not-so-simple knowledge of how to take off, to soar, and to land in a ballet leap or jump was poetically and perceptively analyzed by Edwin Denby, one of America's finest dance critics:

A leap is a whole story with a beginning, a middle and an end . . . . It begins with a knee bend, knees turned out, feet turned out and heels pressed down, to get a surer grip and a smoother flow in the leg action. The bend goes down softly ("as if the body were being sucked into the floor") with a slight accelerando. The thrust upward, the stretch of the legs, is faster than the bend was. The speed of the action must accelerate in a continuous gradation from the beginning of the bend into the final spring upward, so there will be no break in motion when the body leaves the ground . . . . The back muscles have to be kept under the strictest tension to keep the spine erect—the difficulty is to move the pelvis against the spine, instead of the other way around; and as the spine has no material support in the air, you can see that it's like pulling yourself up by your own bootstraps. But that isn't all. The shoulders have to be held rigidly down by main force, so they won't bob upward in the jump. The arms and neck, the hands and head, have to look as comfortable and relaxed as if nothing were happening down below. Really there's as much going on down there as though the arms and head were picnicking on a volcano . . . . But the most obvious test for the dancer comes in the descent from the air, in the recovery from the leap . . . that begins with the speed [of the fall] and progressively diminishes so evenly that you don't notice the transition from the air to the ground. This knee bend slows down as it deepens to what feels like a final rest, though it is only a fraction of a second long . . . . After that, straightening up from the bend must have the feeling of a new start; it is no part of the jump, it is a new breath, a preparation for the next thing.[4]

NOTES

1 Pierre Rameau, *The Dancing Master* (Paris, 1725). Translation by Cyril W. Beaumont (New York: Dance Horizons, 1970), p. 12.

2 Tamara Karsavina, *Classical Ballet: The Flow of Movement* (London: Adam and Charles Black, 1962), p. 68.

3 Gail Grant, *Technical Manual and Dictionary of Classical Ballet* (New York: Dover, 1967), pp. 98–103.

4 Edwin Denby, *Looking at the Dance* (New York: Horizon, 1968), pp. 24–26.

CHAPTER FIVE
ELEMENTS
OF ARTISTRY

*. . . I never take artistry for granted and I am never
satisfied with something being only as good as last
time.*

Erik Bruhn, 1968.[1]

Dancers are rarely, if ever, fully satisfied with their dancing. Improvement is as
important to a ballerina as it is to a beginning student, even though the ballerina
may be striving to enhance the subtle nuances of a step, while the beginner is trying
just to master the step itself. Both searches require diligent work, not merely wishes.
More than that, technical and artistic improvement demand consistent, thoughtful
work. The present chapter offers some ways for the intermediate student to think
about classroom exercises in order to reach beyond basic technique and toward
artistry—the goal of the dance.

**ATTRIBUTES OF
MOVEMENTS**

Every ballet movement, be it an *allegro* step or a *pirouette* in an *adagio*, has
certain inherent elements, essential characteristics defining the movement itself. For
instance, a *sissonne* is a spring into the air from a *demi-plié* on both feet to a landing
in *fondu* on one foot. But, as the intermediate student already knows, even while
a *sissonne* retains those fundamental characteristics, it may vary other attributes in
a great many ways. Four attributes are especially important for any ballet movement:
rhythm, shape, space, and dynamics.

110

"Ballet is about dancing in time"[2] is a simplistic definition, but one containing **RHYTHM** a vital truth. Often many difficulties of performance are overcome simply by correctly understanding the rhythmic structure of a step or combination. Indeed, timing of a movement will affect other attributes, so it must be perceived first. Dancers frequently "talk" a combination, not with such technical terms as *glissade, jeté, pas de bourrée*, and two *changements de pieds*, but with rhythmic syllables ("*ta-tum, TA-tum, ta-ta-tum, tum-tum*"). Sometimes a dance movement must anticipate the beat of the music; other times a movement is enhanced if done after the beat. Once rhythmic structure and accents are clear, attention can turn to other attributes of individual steps and complete combinations.

Because the human body is the medium through which ballet is transmitted to **SHAPE** the viewer, all ballet movements have a human shape—extended, curved, lifted—creating a special balanced design. The dancer's task is to understand the balanced design of each step, pose, or dance phrase, and then try to interpret that shape with his/her individual anatomy. The studio mirror is a valuable aid, but more important are the teacher's eye and the dancer's intelligent use of the body to create an image of balance. As an example, a pose in fifth position right foot front has a pleasing vertical balance when the left arm is *en haut* and the right arm *en bas*. However, if the torso bends in a *cambré* to the right, it requires a greater curve in both arms and a slight lift in the lower arm to enhance the curved balance of the design. The shape of the dancer's attire influences the design taken by the limbs: the romantic tutu, with its bell-shaped skirt, or the tunic with full sleeves, suggest a more rounded shape of the arms in contrast to the streamlined leotard and tights design that encourages more elongated shaping of all limbs. The length of a dancer's own arms will help determine the degree to which they should be curved or extended.

Intrinsically related to the shape of movement is the space in which movement **SPACE** takes place. Obviously, the spatial direction of a step or combination (forward, diagonal, turning, etc.) must be understood clearly, as well as how far in those directions to travel, but there must also be appreciation of the *concept* of space as an arena that always must be filled with harmoniously balanced shape, even during transitions from one step or pose to another. For instance, following a *demi-contretemps* or *failli*, a *piqué en avant* will move the body farther through space, perhaps in order ultimately to display the body in a particular shape, such as *arabesque*. The spatial connection between the completion of the first step (the *demi-contretemps* or *failli*) and the second (the *piqué*) is critical; its importance should not be minimized or ignored. The dancer must be aware of this "in-between" space and carefully shape the body as it moves through it to the *piqué*. Thus, in this example, the arms can lift to *demi-avant* as the head lowers slightly and the back foot points as it passes through for the *piqué*. During this transition movement, the torso must be well lifted even as the supporting leg presses downward in *fondu*. (See Chapter 4, p. 78, third drawing from left, for a similar moment of transition.)

DYNAMICS

The opposing "pulls" just described add dynamics to a transition movement that otherwise can all too easily lose energy and convey collapse instead of anticipation. The ballet vocabulary provides ample opportunity for variety of dynamics, but awareness and use of that variety must be cultivated. To dance (or live) without contrasts is a boring prospect. Soft or sharp, extended or released, quick or slow— and all the gradations in between—are qualities of dynamics to be explored in ballet technique. For instance, in the *glissade* combination mentioned before, each step can have a distinct dynamic quality: the *glissade* glides lightly to the side with arms curved low; the *jeté* thrusts the leading leg sharply into the air, directing the body high off the floor with arms opening strongly outward; the *pas de bourrée* occurs almost as the wink of an eye—quick tiny steps into fifth position as the arms lower; and the two *changements de pieds* emphasize the streamlined verticality of the body as the feet push from the floor, toes sharply pointed downward, arms held low. The final pose, held quietly secure, is in itself a wonderful contrast to the lively steps just preceding it. (For other examples of contrasting dynamics, see Chapter 4.)

FINDING THE PUSH/ SUSTAINING THE IMAGE

Legs and feet propel the dancer from place to place, whether the direction be forward, backward, sideward, or upward. This propulsion almost always involves preparation from a *demi-plié* or *fondu*. If the preparation is from a *plié*, then the force for the movement comes equally and simultaneously from both legs and feet. But when the preparation is from a *fondu*, the push comes from only one leg and foot, often aided by a movement gesture of the raised leg. For example, a *glissade* requires a smooth extension of the opening leg, its foot brushing quickly along the floor until fully pointed, as well as the brisk push-off from the following leg and foot. Thus, the actions of both legs are equally necessary, though not simultaneous, whether the *glissade* be large or small, strong or delicate.

In this and other instances, although the opening or leading leg appears to be initiating the action, the following leg gives the real impetus for the movement. As an example, *piqué tours en dedans* might better be termed *jeté piqué tours*, because a strong push-off from the preparatory *fondu*, as in a *jeté*, is required for a successful turn, rather than just a step onto *demi-pointe*. *Pas de chat* is an example of another step requiring a quick and powerful action by the second leg following the initial lift from the first leg. The beautiful moment when both feet are in *retiré* position *en l'air* is achieved by the carefully timed push-off from the second leg, occurring while the first leg continues to lift to its highest point.

More complicated steps require more coordinated movements and timing from the rest of the body. The arms play a special role in these cases. For instance, in a *sissonne retombée* (a combination of a *sissonne ouverte de coté* with a *coupé* and *assemblé*), the timing and lift of the arms provide the suspension necessary for the aerial quality of the step. During the push into the air for the *sissonne*, the arms must lift to a fairly high position *en avant* (or even *en haut*) and momentarily sustain that pose before opening *à la seconde* at the last possible moment for the completion of the *sissonne* in *fondu*. This tiny hesitation of *port de bras* provides the buoyancy necessary to sustain the body longer in the air. (See Chapter 4, pp. 82–84, for more discussion of this step.)

The general principles of sustained *port de bras* are applicable in numerous other steps, such as *ballotté, tour jeté,* and *fouetté en l'air.* In the latter step, the brilliancy of the *fouetté* turn in the air is enhanced (and the body is better controlled) if the arms, having been brought *en haut*, remain overhead until *after* the turn is completed before opening outward to the landing pose.

A simple example can be found in *port de bras* for *soubresaut*—and also *soussus*—even if the arms are to remain low. As the elevation begins, a *bras bas* position can be raised very slightly, including a minute lift of the hands from the wrists. Not only does the dancer's body respond to this almost imperceptible lift, but so also does the viewer sense greater suspension in the jump or *relevé*. In other words, the arms do not have to ascend always overhead in such springs or rises; much the same effect can be gained from a more subtle *port de bras*.

Perhaps the most subtle suspension occurs in the torso during a *plié* or *fondu*; when the dancer goes down, the body must "think" up, even while the legs release into the preparatory or finishing bend. It is almost as if the body were divided into two halves—from waist down pressing into the floor, but from waist up resisting that pull by lifting higher.

The lift, turn, incline, or lowering of the head also enhances any movement. The sheer weight of the head (about ten pounds) assures it an important role, and this role must be appreciated. The slight anticipatory movement of the head can direct the rest of the body toward the position of balance (as in a *piqué en avant*) or elevation (as in a *grand jeté*), or emphasis (as in a *temps de cuisse*). In the latter example, the head can lower slightly during the preparatory *retiré* or *dégagé*, then lift quickly with the *sissonne*, thus emphasizing the sudden spring into the air.

Perhaps the greatest misuse of the head occurs during the typical first exercise of class, the *grands pliés*. All too often, as the body lowers, the head falls forward, pulling shoulders and torso out of alignment. A more efficient movement would be: a slight turn of the head toward the open arm as the *plié* begins, a focus forward with head straight as the body descends in the *plié*, a slight turn of the head toward the barre as the body ascends, and a return of focus toward the opening arm as the legs straighten.

GRAND PLIÉ

**MOVEMENT
ECONOMY**

The very notion of a "classical" technique implies observation of tradition, simplicity, and control as opposed to novelty, ornamentation, and lack of restraint. A ballet student can cultivate this economical classical image from the very first exercise at barre. In addition to the simple use of the head suggested above, the use of the legs in changing positions of the feet should be simple also. For instance, for *plié* exercises, the position at the barre should be such that only the outside foot need move in order to change from first to second position, or from second to fifth position, and so on, rather than a constant shifting of both feet as each new position is assumed. If and when it *is* necessary to move the inside foot to help establish a new position, it should be done deliberately—the foot pointing and closing smoothly, avoiding the distracting "shuffle of feet and wiggle of hips" coming into a new position. When positions are changed, there is no need for the head to lower, eyes searching for the foot; the foot *will* move to a new position *without* being watched by the mover.

The enormous energy required of the ballet dancer demands efficient use of that energy. Extraneous movement can be debilitating to the performer as well as confusing to the viewer. Perhaps at no time is efficiency more important or impressive than in the beginning and ending of a dance phrase. To stand quietly ready, then take the one essential movement necessary, or to complete a phrase without unnecessary additional movements, are marks of the dance artist. A prime instance is the taking of *demi-plié*, ballet's most basic motion and the one most often maligned. As a preparation and/or finish for a movement, the *demi-plié* should be one smooth bending action, not several little bounces. If ankles and feet release sufficiently as the heels press downward, the awkward stuttering effect of a preparatory or terminating *demi-plié* can be avoided. Of course, the individual anatomical design of an ankle may or may not facilitate this action, but in all instances, a concentrated determination not to bounce must be made. Similarly, a *demi-pointe* position must be securely taken—toes pressing against the floor and ankles firmly placed—so that the balance is not disturbed by a wavering of the feet. Again, efficiency of movement is the goal.

Seemingly opposed to the concept of movement economy or efficiency is the notion of movement embellishment. But here embellishment does not connote ornamentation or "fanciness," rather, simple enhancement of movement, often accomplished merely by a judicious incline of the head or a timing of *port de bras*, as already suggested. Even during barre exercises, the incline or turn of the head toward the forward leg establishes a lovely dance image in keeping with the harmony of classical ballet. The slight incline and lowering of the head during a preparatory *fondu*, then the lifting and turning of the head during the ensuing *développé en relevé* is another example of simple embellishment that adds to the effectiveness of the total action. (See Chapter 2 for additional movements of the head in barre exercises.)

EMBELLISH-MENT OF MOVEMENT

Already noted is the critical role played by the action of the arms before and during a step or phrase. One more simple instance, having to do with the completion of a movement, is worth mention here. For example, following the extension of a leg to a given direction, perhaps *écarté devant*, allow the arms to ever so slightly extend and lift, then begin to lower them before the leg changes its level. After the arms have initiated the action, allow the lowering of the arms and leg to finish simultaneously. The resulting pleasant image is one of sustained control.

**THREE-
DIMENSIONAL
IMAGE**

Displaying the three dimensions of the body—height, width, and depth—in balanced designs is one of the hallmarks of ballet technique, especially pleasing in poses toward the diagonal (see also Chapter 3, p. 48). Achieving a harmonious design of curved arms, inclined head, and straight extended leg in diagonal positions is a dancer's ceaseless quest. It may be helpful to think of the arms in those poses as having both an "outer" and an "inner" design. In the pose *croisé derrière*, for instance, as the downstage arm curves overhead, consider not only the outer curve made by that arm, but also the inner curve and its shape relationship with the neck and head.

Correct   Incorrect

Correct   Incorrect

That inner design—the space between the arm, head, and neck—must have a clearly defined shape just as important as the shape of the limbs themselves. Sometimes called negative space (implying the area described by, but not filled with, the body), this area is molded constantly by the dancer's movements. A common and important negative space is the area between the back arm and the leg extended in *arabesque*. If the space is squeezed, or too wide, the harmony of the *arabesque* line is reduced accordingly (see also Chapter 3, pp. 54–56).

A *retiré* or *cou-de-pied* position molds another important inner shape, the triangular space between the straight supporting leg and the bent raised leg. The student will become aware of many other examples.

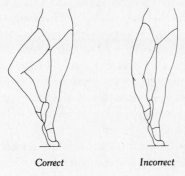

Correct   *Incorrect*

Using the limbs of the body to mold or shape space is not a common balletic concept, but it is effective, nevertheless.

NEGLECTED BASICS

Walking and running seem so elementary they are seldom deemed worthy of practice, while actually they are far from simple and deserve classroom attention. Rehearsal periods or performances are not places to learn to feel comfortable in the balletic stylization of those basic locomotions. Nor should their practice be omitted from a nonprofessional student's ballet education. A great deal of time need not be spent in such practice, but occasional use in classroom combinations will begin to dispel awkwardness or self-consciousness.

It is not necessary to begin this practice by having to walk or run the full length of the studio, sometimes an unnerving experience. Instead, a few slow walking steps may be included in a *port de bras* or an *adagio* combination. For example, beginning in fifth position *croisé* right foot front, lift the left foot into a very small *retiré*, pointed foot passing closely by the supporting ankle, and step forward onto the left quarter-point. Quickly and softly lower the heel, immediately transferring the weight completely over the straight left leg. Repeat the movement with the right foot. The step forward need not be completely turned-out, but its placement should correspond to an open fourth position (opposite first instead of fifth position). The arms might open gradually *en avant*, and then to *croisé devant*, during a series of steps foward.

A *port de bras* or *adagio* sequence could continue from this point. The steps might also be practiced in an individual circle, perhaps taking four steps to produce a turn from one downstage corner to the other.

Quicker walking steps, or a combination of first slow, then quick steps can add dynamics to dance phrases. The quicker steps usually are done with less turn-out and on the balls of the feet without the heels lowering to the floor. Whether slow or quick, the steps should be done without sliding or shuffling the feet. Each foot should be placed distinctly and quietly, with the toes touching the ground before the heel.

Still quicker walks or runs can be effective in *allegro* combinations, particularly as preparations for large jumps or as finishes to a dance phrase. Before the run begins, the body should lift slightly, inhaling as if in anticipation of the quick forward movement. For instance, this can occur with a rise to *demi-pointes* in fifth position or with a small step backward and then a *petit développé en avant en relevé* with the other leg. Either preparation encourages a lighter, swifter run than does just stepping forward from a flat position. As the speed of the run increases, it causes the little *retirés* of the feet and the turn-out to almost disappear.

Types of runs vary according to circumstance and performer. A dance phrase for a female dancer may require rapid, tiny steps executed in a parallel first position on *demi-pointes* with the feet thrown slightly forward, almost as in a travelling *passe-pied*. In another context, a male dancer might take longer, deeper strides with more turn-out.

**DANCING ON
POINT**

Toe dancing, or "point work," as it is called, fascinates both the dance student and dance observer. When done correctly, it is a pleasure to both, but if done incorrectly it is not only painful to do and to see, but can be damaging to the feet, ankles, knees, and back of the performer. Therefore, its study must be done carefully, intelligently, and at the right time.

In most instances, the bones of the feet have not hardened enough before age twelve to sustain the demands of point work. Beyond that age, its study should be undertaken only after the student has attained a strong basic technique. A correctly placed body is particularly important. These two factors—strength and placement—usually require several years of serious ballet study several days a week. One or two classes per week, even continued over a number of years, is usually insufficient preparation for point work. Ideally, the student takes classes daily before attempting point work because:

> It cannot be too strongly stressed that *pointe* work is the end result of slow gradual training of the whole body, back, hips, thighs, legs, feet, coordination of movement and the "placing" of the body, so that the weight is lifted upwards off the feet, with straight knees, perfect balance, with a perfect *demi-pointe*, and without any tendency on the part of the feet to sickle either in or out or the toes to curl or clutch.[3]

Although the entire body must be ready for point work (even the head must be poised correctly), the feet present special considerations. Ideally they should have sturdy, compact arches rather than high, flexible ones. Short toes of almost equal length are preferable to long or tapering toes, because balance on point is taken on the pads of the toes just beyond the nails. Thus, the point position is one in which the toes are straight (never knuckled over or released backward) and in a direct line under the ankle.

POINT SHOES

It should be apparent by now that the point shoe itself is not the secret to point work, but rather an aid to the body's own strength. Today's shoes, much stronger than those used by early-nineteenth-century ballerinas (see Chapter 6, pp. 130–131), nevertheless are merely satin-covered cloth slippers, with very narrow leather soles and a "box" made up only of about seven layers of cloth held together by a particular kind of glue. This very lightweight shoe breaks down quickly; a professional dancer may need several pairs for one evening's performance. Expert guidance is needed for the initial fitting and selection of shoe style (lighter "box," stronger sole, higher vamp, etc.). When trying on shoes, the student should be sure her toenails have been trimmed closely, because a long nail may alter the fit and feel of the shoes. She should wear tights of the thickness ordinarily worn with the shoes.

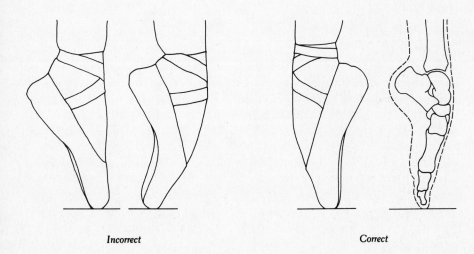

Incorrect   *Correct*

Preparation of the shoes for wear—that is, just where and how the ribbons are sewn on, if and where elastic is attached at the heel, how much the "box" and sole are softened before the shoe is actually worn—is highly individual.

ELEMENTARY EXERCISES

Introduction to point work begins at the barre with elementary exercises based on the two ways of getting onto point: the *relevé*, or rise up to point, and the *posé*, or step directly onto point. The *relevé* is done either smoothly or sharply, that is, it can be a sustained rise, an almost rolling-up and rolling-down action through the entire foot, or it can be a very small spring from *demi-plié* onto a fully stretched foot. The sustained rise requires more strength and control, and it can be a difficult movement for the highly arched, flexible foot. The springing *relevé* requires a firm push-off from the heels in *demi-plié* and a quick spring, not jump, onto full point and then a return to *demi-plié* by another very slight spring. The *posé* directly onto point requires a strong *fondu* and push-off from the supporting leg and an already strongly arched extended foot. The same action when done quickly and sharply is often called *piqué*.

Some elementary point exercises done at barre include:

RELEVÉS ONTO TWO FEET

Relevés, springing or sustained: rise and lower, as described above, in first, second, and fifth position, and later in fourth position with *épaulement*. (In the springing *relevés* the toes typically move closer together on the rise, and return to place on the *demi-plié*. Thus, the springing *relevé* in fifth position is a *soussus*, one foot directly in back of the other on point.)

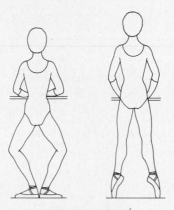 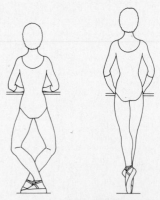

SUSTAINED RELEVÉ
IN FIRST POSITION

SPRINGING RELEVÉ (SOUSSUS)
IN FIFTH POSITION

120

**ELEMENTS OF
ARTISTRY**

Echappé Relevé: spring from fifth position *demi-plié* to second position *sur les pointes*, and return, with or without change of feet, to fifth position *demi-plié*. Later spring to fourth position, and return to fifth.

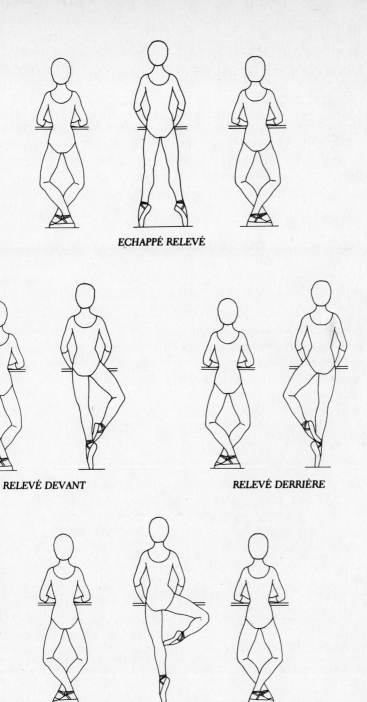

ECHAPPÉ RELEVÉ

RELEVÉ DEVANT

RELEVÉ DERRIÈRE

RELEVÉ PASSÉ DESSOUS

RELEVÉS ONTO ONE FOOT

Relevé Devant: spring from fifth position *demi-plié* onto the point of the back foot as the front foot is raised in front of the ankle or knee, and return both feet simultaneously to *demi-plié*. Reverse the pattern for *relevé derrière*.

Relevé Passé: spring from fifth position *demi-plié* onto the point of the back foot as the front foot is raised to the side of the supporting knee, and lower it behind (*dessous*) as both feet close simultaneously to fifth position *demi-plié*. Reverse the pattern for *relevé passé dessus*.

POSÉS (PIQUÉS)

Piqué en Arrière: fondu on the front leg as the back foot rises and arches behind the supporting ankle, and step directly onto the point of the back foot. *Fondu*, either by stepping onto the foot that was raised, or by lowering through *demi-pointe* to the heel of the foot that was on point. Reverse the pattern for *piqué en avant*.

Glissade: demi-plié in fifth position, slide one foot *à la seconde* just off the floor. Push from the supporting leg, step directly onto the point of the extended foot, and immediately close the other foot to fifth position *en pointes*. Lower both feet to *demi-plié* fifth position. This may be done with or without a change of feet on the close to fifth position.

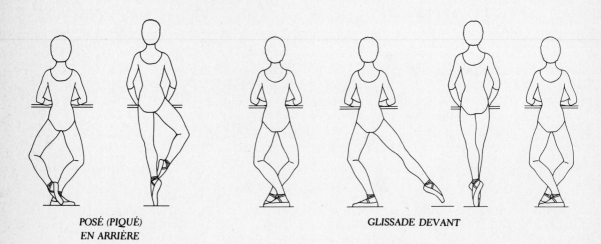

POSÉ (PIQUÉ)
EN ARRIÈRE

GLISSADE DEVANT

Pas de Bourrée Dessous: stand on the right foot with the left foot arched behind the supporting leg. *Fondu* on the right leg, and step in place directly onto the left point, immediately raising the right foot *sur le cou-de-pied devant*. Step toward the right side onto the right point, and raise the left foot *sur le cou-de-pied devant*. Lower the left foot in place in *fondu*, immediately raising the right foot *sur le cou-de-pied derrière*. Reverse the pattern for *pas de bourrée dessus*. (The raised foot may be lifted higher to a *retiré* position each time, and the close of the third step may be to fifth position *en pointes* before the finish *en fondu*.)

Bourrée Couru or *Pas de Bourrée Couru:* begin in fifth position either with a *demi-plié* and *soussus* onto the points, or with a *fondu* and step onto the point of the back foot, as in the above combination. Take a series of tiny steps, traveling in the direction of the front foot, keeping the feet fully stretched but allowing a slight release of the knee as the foot is picked up. Keep the legs well crossed and turned-out so the image of fifth position is retained. This is easier if the travel of the *bourrée* is initiated by the back foot; it should move well behind the front foot as though pushing it along, rather than the front foot stepping out first, thus opening space between the legs. *Bourrée couru* can be practiced in place, before traveling to the side.

PAS DE BOURRÉE DESSOUS   BOURRÉE COURU

Once exercises such as these are learned at barre, they are practiced in center floor. Eventually, almost all *demi-pointe* steps are transferred to full point. Later, even certain jumps, such as *sissonne ouvert* or *changement de pieds*, are done on point. All turns on *demi-pointe*, whether from a *relevé* or a *posé*, can become turns *en pointe*.

Customarily, point work is practiced during the last part of the lesson. Students are asked to change from ballet shoes to point shoes and return to the barre for elementary exercises. Gradually more time is given to point work so that center combinations can be included. Later, one entire class each week is given *en pointe*. Most advanced and professional dancers wear old point shoes to all ballet classes, often having removed the heavier inner sole to lighten the shoe. In this way, they are saved the expense of buying soft ballet slippers for class, and they grow accustomed to working in point shoes.

Sometimes teachers advise male students to exercise on point in order to strengthen their feet, and also to familiarize themselves with point technique. This is especially helpful for men aspiring to teach. The reasons men have not danced *en pointe* are artistic not anatomical. Romantic ballet scenarios of the nineteenth century frequently depicted woman in the role of unattainable, unearthly spirit and man in the role of haplessly beguiled mortal. It was logical for women in those roles of sylphs or wilis to try to defy gravity, to rise to toe tip before "flying" away (and often dancers were flown, lifted by wires attached to their bodices). There was no artistic justification for men to do so.

USING THE EYES

Of all the elements of artistry that might be discussed, perhaps none is more important than the use of the eyes. Obviously, the eyes are the tools by which a student learns—watching a teacher demonstrate, observing other students practicing, checking one's own image in the mirror. Also, the focus of the eyes helps direct movement in traveling and turning steps, serving to orient the dancer in space. A clear focus can help maintain balance, whether standing or spotting for turns. But the eyes are also a prime means of communicating, and therefore they must be expressive. Blank stares or downcast eyes can destroy the beauty and effectiveness of a dance phrase as surely as any other error. For a performer, few things are as unsettling as dancing with someone who looks past, not directly at, you. An audience can detect this lack of eye communication. Classroom combinations need to emphasize expressive focus of the eyes, thus training another important area of the body.

Becoming aware of the elements of artistry is one of the rewards, as well as one of the challenges, of ballet beyond the basics. These remarks from a student sum it up:

> As I enter my third year of ballet training, the little things are becoming more important in improving the quality of my dancing. When I began dancing, it was very easy to get better. If I could do a *glissade* or a *pas de bourrée* at all, then I was good—for Ballet One. Now that I've advanced, perhaps by default, to Intermediate Ballet, mastering more new moves isn't as important as it once was. A shift in emphasis has begun from bigger and more enthusiastic to cleaner and more aesthetic.

From a ballet student's essay at the University of Hawaii, 1980.

NOTES

1 Lydia Joel "Erik Bruhn and Stockholm," *Dance Magazine*, Vol. 42, No. 9 (September, 1968), p. 48. Erik Bruhn, trained in the Bournonville tradition, is recognized as one of the finest dancers of his time, both for his performances as a member of the Royal Danish Ballet, and as a guest artist with companies around the world.

2 Lincoln Kirstein, "What Ballet Is About: An American Glossary," *Dance Perspectives*, Vol. 1 (Winter, 1959), p. 80.

3 Celia Sparger, *Anatomy and Ballet*, (London: Adam and Charles Black, 4th ed. 1965), p. 74.

Anatole Vilzak, *partnering Olga Spessivtzeva in* Swan Lake *at the Maryinsky Theatre in the first quarter of this century, has vividly continued the ballet tradition by teaching the foremost dancers and students of the Ballet Russe de Monte Carlo School (1949–51), the American Ballet Theatre School (1951–63), the Washington School of Ballet (1963–66), and the San Francisco Ballet School (1966 to present). See current photograph, Chapter 1, p. 11. Courtesy, Mr. Vilzak.*

CHAPTER SIX
LEARNING FROM HISTORY

Times change, taste changes; many of the strings that once resounded so delightfully are broken now or out of tune.

August Bournonville, 1877.[1]

Lacking a universally accepted recording device, such as the musical score, ballet, more than most arts, has had to rely on interpersonal contact for the study, transmission, and preservation of its technique and repertory. Despite the occasional success of various notation systems, from *Chorégraphie*, published in Paris in 1700 by Raoul Anger Feuillet, to the twentieth-century methods of Rudolf Benesh and Rudolf von Laban, to contemporary videotape and film, ballet's rich traditions continue to be passed along primarily as they always have been, from individual to individual. Teacher and student, choreographer and cast, professional and beginner—all are personally engaged in transmitting and preserving, through mind and muscles, a complex art form. Thus, ballet's technical literature and choreographic scores are relatively scarce, as compared with other arts such as music and drama. Indeed, a book on ballet technique, such as this one, meets active resistance from some who insist that dance must be done, not discussed. However, one use of a technical manual is to preserve, in another way, some of ballet's traditions as they are practiced in the classrooms. This chapter offers a glimpse backward, a chance to contemplate exercises and combinations performed in earlier classrooms, as notated and/or described by past ballet masters. The sources are a precious few, but perhaps from the work of these men we can gain a richer understanding of ballet's technical history and an enrichment for our own technical training.

A NEW LOOK AT AN OLD BARRE

The earliest description of the format for a ballet lesson appears in a small manual published in 1820 in Milan, *Traité Elémentaire, Théorique et Pratique de l'Art de la Danse*[2] (An Elementary Treatise upon the Theory and Practice of the Art of Dancing) written by a young Neapolitan-born dancer, Carlo Blasis, who later became a leading teacher in Europe. His lesson, no doubt based on practices long in use, begins with the "elementary exercises" practiced at the barre and later repeated in center floor "without support."

THE *PLIÉS*

As today, barre work began with *pliés*, and in Blasis' class they were done in all five positions of the feet, including third position. In all *pliés*, the dancer was instructed to practice "bending the knees without lifting the heel from the ground."[3] Thus, *grand plié* was not included as a regular feature of practice and certainly not as a first exercise. Probably *grands pliés* entered the curriculum in response to choreographic use (such as in the nineteenth-century Bournonville ballets, which occasionally feature *assemblé* finishing in a deep *grand plié*). According to Blasis' contemporary, Paris Opera ballet instructor G. Léopold Adice,[4] the barre sequence called for three slow *pliés* followed by three quick ones in each position.

THE *BATTEMENTS*

Next in the lesson came the *grands battements*, "performed by raising the fully extended leg to the height of the hip."[5] Higher *battements* and extensions are relatively recent additions to ballet technique, becoming commonplace only by the mid-twentieth century and usually practiced toward the end of the barre sequence.

Blasis' students were required to perform 16 *grands battements* to the front, first with the right leg and then with the left. The same number were repeated in each direction, alternating legs after each 16 *battements*, for a total of 128! Interestingly, the *battements à la seconde* did not alternate closing front and back in fifth position, but rather were closed in front each time for the first series (sixteen with the right leg, then sixteen with the left), then closed in back (16 times with each leg). Such practice seems to prevent an all-too-common fault of twisting in the turn-out in order to alternate closings from second to fifth position. This practice of not alternating the closing is even more clearly stated by an English ballet master and author of the same period, E. A. Théleur.[6] The same practice was observed when performing the next exercise, known today as *battements tendus*. Executed in double time,[7] presumably to that of the *grands battements*, these *battements* totalled 48 for each leg.

Students in the early nineteenth century were instructed to keep their heels firmly on the ground in all pliés. *Blasis,* Code of Terpsichore, *Plate II, figure 4. Courtesy of Dance Horizon republication.*

The appropriate height for grand battement *in the nineteenth century was hip level. Blasis,* Code of Terpsichore, *Plate II, figure 5. Courtesy of Dance Horizon republication.*

THE *RONDS DE JAMBE*

Descriptions of *rond de jambe à terre* emphasize that it must begin and end in second position *pointe tendue*. The subtle but distinctive message is the opening to second position for the *completion* of each circle. Performed with due attention, this detail gives a clear awareness of turning outward from the hip during each arc. The number to be performed is again impressive: thirty-two *en dehors* with each leg, followed by thirty-two *en dedans*.

Ronds de jambe en l'air were practiced with the supporting foot flat, as well as on *demi-pointe*. Théleur advocates that "a circle should be described as large as possible, taking care at the same time, as soon as the thigh is placed in its proper position, never to move the hip joint, the place of action being only at the knee."[8] He goes on to say the *ronds de jambe* should be done "commencing slowly, and gradually increasing their velocity."[9] Adice recalls the total number as 128, *en dehors* and *en dedans*, in Blasis' classes.

THE *PETITS BATTEMENTS*

The little *battements* on the instep, or *petits battements sur le cou-de-pied*, were to be practiced slowly and well pronounced with each leg, then with increasing speed ". . . until you can perform them as rapidly as you can count."[10] Possibly the thirty-two slower *battements*, which provided ". . . great play and increased strength at the insteps and joints of the toes," resembled our *battements frappés*, while the sixty rapid *battements* were identical with our *petits battements sur le cou-de-pied*. Apparently, both kinds of *battements* were first practiced with the supporting foot flat, then "with the body resting on the ball of the foot that is not in action."[11] Note that the illustration of *cou-de-pied* calls for the heel positioned slightly above and forward of the supporting ankle and the toes stretched well downward but not wrapped around to the back.

Such were the "elementary exercises"—a total of 648 leg movements at barre, then repeated in center floor! The only other barre exercise mentioned is the practice of rising to the toes. Blasis' illustrations show only a high three-quarter point, but Théleur often specifies and illustrates positions on the "points of the toes." To perform the rise to toe-tip properly, Théleur advises keeping ". . . the joints of the toes perfectly straight from the commencement of the movement."[12] This is a clear indication of the new dimension dance was reaching in the early nineteenth century: Théleur wrote in 1831; the first romantic ballet, *La Sylphide*, appeared the following year, and its star, Marie Taglioni, danced *en pointe*. The strength she had gained through rigorous daily training (two-hour classes, three times a day) allowed her to rise to toe-tip, for her shoes were neither blocked nor reinforced, but only lightly darned around the edges. Although Taglioni was not the first to dance on point, her ethereal performance as the Sylph established the importance of the new style.

In a Spanish dance, the Cachucha, Marie Taglioni impressed a London observer as "the very soul of swiftness" with her "succession of flying movements . . . in the midst of which she alights on the point of her feet, with a look over her shoulder . . . like a deer standing with expanded nostril and neck uplifted to its loftiest height." The dance occurred in the ballet La Gitana, choreographed in 1839 by her father, Filippo Taglioni. The painting of Taglioni dancing the Cachucha was done that same year by the English artist Joseph Rubens Powell. Courtesy, Russell Hartley and the Archives for the Performing Arts, Mill Valley, California.

The position of the foot on the instep or sur le cou-de-pied, *shown here with the supporting foot on a very high three-quarter point, was a favorite position for pirouettes.* Blasis, Code of Terpsichore, *Plate IX, figure 4. Courtesy of Dance Horizon republication.*

Dancing on the points of the toes was the most revolutionary technical development of the early nineteenth century. The first illustration of this accomplishment to appear in a technical manual was 1831 in Théleur, Letters on Dancing, Plate 20. Collection of Regine Astier, 1832 edition.

Following repetition of all the barre exercises in center floor, students in the early-nineteenth-century classes practiced a step sequence inherited from their ballet predecessors a century before, the *temps de courant*.[13] In the classes of Filippo Taglioni, Marie's father and principal teacher, this sequence always preceded more complicated center work because it prepared ". . . the arms, the body, and especially the hips, the knees, and the insteps for the steps of balance which were to follow."[14] It seems a pity that the *temps de courant* disappeared from the classroom (according to Adice, by 1859, the sequence was seldom used except in children's classes), but thanks to Théleur's description and system of notation these steps can be revived.

TEMPS DE COURANT SINGLE (or *Simple*)[15]

Measure	Count	
		From fifth position, right foot behind:
	and	*demi-plié*;
1.	*one*	rise to *demi-pointe*, brushing the right foot *à la seconde*;
	two	staying on the left *demi-pointe*, carry the right leg in an arc to the front (like a *demi-rond de jambe*);
	three	step forward onto the right foot, lowering the heel;
	and	slide the left foot into fifth position back in *demi-plié*.
2.	*one, two, three*	Repeat to the other side.

The exercise can be repeated from the beginning, then reversed to travel backward.

TEMPS DE COURANT DOUBLE (or *Composé*)

Measure	Count	
		From fifth position, right foot behind:
	and	*demi-plié*;
1.	*one*	rise to *demi-pointe*, brushing the right foot *à la seconde*;
	and	lower both heels and *demi-plié* in second position;
	two	rise to *demi-pointe* on the left foot, raising the right leg again to the side before carrying it in an arc to the front;
	three	step forward onto the right foot, lowering the heel;
	and	slide the left foot into fifth position back in *demi-plié*.
2.	*one, two, three*	Repeat to the other side.

The exercise can be repeated from the beginning, then reversed to travel backward.

134

Unfortunately, Théleur's notation system does not provide descriptions of arm movements with the exercise, but Adice rescues the situation somewhat by telling us that the *temps de courant simple* is accompanied by rounded movements of the arms *en dehors* and *en dedans*. Thus, perhaps, when traveling forward, the arm opposite the extending leg is carried from a low position to a forward or high position, then out to the side. When traveling backward, one arm is carried from a low position outward to the side, then either forward or overhead. During each *temps de courant double*, both arms move at the same time but in opposite directions, according to Adice.[16] A variety of *port de bras* might be tried, in the spirit of "preparing for the work which is to follow." But bear in mind the conventions of an earlier style: "In raising the arms, when the body is in a front position, care should be taken never to permit the hands to approach each other, so as to hide the body; they should rise in front, opposite the shoulders."[17] Thus, as the manual illustrations testify, arms were more rounded and hands farther apart in the *bras bas*, *bras avant* (sometimes termed *bras arrondis*), and *bras haut* position than in today's technique.

The early-nineteenth-century lesson proceeded with the *coupés*, movements quite different from those today bearing the same name. For a description of an exercise of *coupés*, including timing and *port de bras*, we turn to Arthur Michel Saint-Léon, dancer, teacher, choreographer (*Coppélia*, 1870, was his most famous ballet), violinist, and author of yet another system of dance notation.

COUPÉ EN AVANT ET EN ARRIÈRE[18] (16 measures of 4/4, *andante*)

Measure	Count	
		From *pointe tendue*, right foot *à la seconde*, *bras bas*:
1.	*one*	close the right foot to first position in *demi-plié*;
	two	immediately extend the right leg forward to 45 degrees while remaining in *fondu* on the left;
	three	step forward onto the right *demi-pointe*, bringing the left foot *sur le cou-de-pied derrière*;
	four	lower the right heel and raise the left leg to *attitude à la seconde* at 45 degrees, *bras arrondis*[19];
2.	*one* through *four*	Slowly continue to develop the leg to 90 degrees *à la seconde*, *bras à la seconde*, rising to *demi-pointe* on the right foot.
3. and 4.	*one* through *eight*	During the next two measures, make one complete turn *en dehors* to the left, keeping the left leg at hip level *à la seconde*. (The notation does not indicate a lowering of the heel during the slow turn, but intermediate students may be advised to do so.) At the completion of the turn, lower the left leg to 45 degrees, *bras bas*.
1.–4.	*one* through *sixteen*	Close to first position to begin the entire sequence to the other side.
1.–8.	*one* through *thirty-two*	Reverse the entire sequence by stepping backward, raising the foot *sur le cou-de-pied devant*, and turning *en dedans*. Following the final turn, lower the right leg to third position back, body facing downstage right, *bras bas*.

EXEMPLE 9ème

The exercise Coupé en avant et en arrière, *mentioned by several early-nineteenth-century dancing masters, was notated in 1852 by Saint-Léon in his* La Sténochorégraphie.

The continuity of ballet technique, in spite of inevitable change, is illustrated nicely by the next exercise, the *grand fouetté*. As early as 1820, Blasis lists *grand fouetté* "facing and while turning," and in the next decade Théleur notates a version of *fouetté* finishing in an *attitude* that strongly resembles a more complicated version by Saint-Léon in 1852. And the descriptions and notations by Saint-Léon seem to correspond to the *grands fouettés de face* and *en tournant* discussed by Adice seven years later. Of perhaps greater interest are the striking similarities between these exercises and the first part of Cecchetti's *Grand Fouetté Adage,*[20] as well as the Italian *grand fouetté* described by Vaganova in 1934.[21]

Here we will follow Saint-Léon's version, using his terminology of *corps gauche* (body facing downstage left corner) and *corps droit* (body facing downstage right corner) to indicate diagonal poses.

GRAND FOUETTÉ LENT, POSÉ ATTITUDE[22] (8 measures of 4/4, adagio)

Measure	Count	
		From fifth position, right foot front, *corps gauche, bras bas:*
	and	*retiré devant* with the right leg, rising to *demi-pointe* on the left foot, as the body turns right toward the downstage right corner;
1.	*one and two*	*fondu* on the left leg as the right leg opens to *attitude devant*, left arm *arrondi* and right arm *à la seconde;*
	three and four	straighten the left knee and carry the right leg *à la seconde*, rising to *demi-pointe* as the body inclines slightly away from the raised leg, right arm *haut*, left arm *à la seconde.*
2.	*one and two*	Without pause continue to rotate the body left to face downstage left, carrying the right leg to *attitude effacée derrière* as the left leg lowers in *fondu*, right arm remaining in *attitude;*[23]
	three and four	*retiré* with the right leg as the body turns right again toward the downstage right corner, *bras bas.*
3.	*one and two*	*Fondu* on the left leg as the right leg opens to *attitude devant, bras arrondis;*
	three and four	remain in *fondu* as the right leg straightens, *bras à la seconde.*
4.	*one*	*Posé* forward onto the right *demi-pointe*, raising the left leg to *attitude effacée derrière*, left arm *haut;*
	two	*fondu* on the right leg;
	three	*relevé* in the same position;
	four	*retiré* with the left leg as the body turns left toward the downstage left corner, *bras bas.*
1.–4.	*one* through *sixteen*	Repeat the entire sequence to the other side. Following the final *relevé en attitude*, lower the right leg to third position back, *corps droit, bras bas.*

Saint-Léon goes on to describe and notate a more difficult version of *grand fouetté lent* with turns *en dehors en attitude*. Here it might be mentioned that, although the examples of *adage* exercises described by these early masters were not long or overly complicated, they were numerous and were repeated several times, thus requiring and, no doubt, building considerable strength and endurance.

These nineteenth-century manuals make no mention of bending or stretching exercises, yet their drawings (Blasis, Théleur) and notation (Saint-Léon) depict far greater mobility for the torso than was used in eighteenth-century dancing, when verticality was imposed by stiff corsets. Dancers of the nineteenth century, with less bulky costuming and lighter corsets with fewer stays, were able to incline the body into more horizontal positions. For examples of bending and stretching exercises we now turn to a relatively unknown ballet master of the late nineteenth and early twentieth centuries, Rafaele Grassi.

Marie Sallé, a ballerina of the early eighteenth century, is pictured in typical costuming of her day. Compare her pose and dress with those of Taglioni and Spessivtzeva one and two centuries later. Engraving by Nicolas de Larmessin from the painting by Nicolas Lancret (1690–1743). Author's collection.

From fifth position, right foot back, *bras bas:*

(A)   *pointe tendue à la seconde* with the right foot, *bras arrondis;* raise the left arm
         haut as the right arm opens à la seconde;
      cambré sideward to the left, keeping the arms in their same relationship to the
         torso;
      straighten the torso to the upright position, opening the left arm à la seconde;
      close the right foot to fifth position front, *bras bas.*
      Repeat to the other side.

(B)   *pointe tendue à la seconde* with the right foot, arms rising as in exercise A;
      turn the torso to the right, rotating only at the waist, and begin a *cambré*
         backward, bending the left elbow so that the left hand passes by the face,
         and deepen the *cambré*, extending the left arm, hand toward the ceiling;

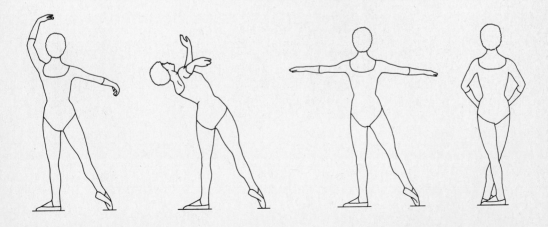

straighten the torso to the upright position, passing the left arm *arrondi* and
then *à la seconde*;

close the right foot to fifth position front, *bras bas*.

Repeat to the other side.

(C) *pointe tendue à la seconde* with the right foot, *bras arrondis* and then *à la
seconde*;

fondu on the supporting leg and, keeping the hips *de face* as much as possible,
turn the torso in the direction of the extended leg, and bend forward from
the waist toward the extended leg, *bras arrondi*;

straighten the knee and the torso to the upright position, *bras haut*;

cambré sideward to the left, keeping the relationship of the arms overhead;

straighten the torso to the upright position, *bras à la seconde*;

close the right foot to fifth position front, *bras bas*.

Repeat to the other side.

(D)   *pointe tendue à la seconde* with the right foot, *bras arrondis* and then right
        arm *haut* as the left arm opens *à la seconde*;
      fondu on the supporting leg and, keeping the hips *de face* as much as possible,
        turn the torso in the direction of the extended leg, and bend slightly forward
        from the waist toward the extended leg, allowing the right elbow to bend
        so that the right hand passes by the face; continue to deepen the bend
        forward, and extend the right hand toward the pointed foot;
      straighten the supporting knee and the torso to the upright position, *bras à la
        seconde*, right arm slightly raised;
      close the right foot to fifth position front, *bras bas*.
      Repeat to the other side.

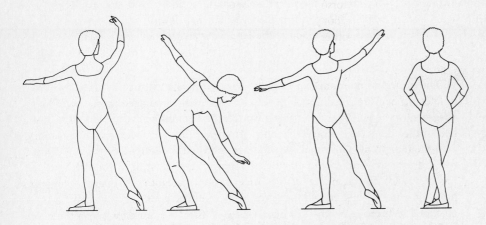

The entire series (A, B, C, D) can now be reversed, beginning with the left
leg and closing fifth position back each time.

Another exercise from Saint-Léon, a brief combination with a very long title,
offers a nice challenge and preparation for *allegro*.

TEMPS DE COU-DE-PIED, PAS MARCHÉ EN AVANT, ATTITUDE POSÉ DERRIÈRE, ET CHANGEMENT DE PIED, EN AVANT ET EN ARRIÈRE[25] (17 measures of 3/4, *moderato*)

Measure	Count	
1.*	one	Hold fifth position, right foot front, *corps guache, bras bas*;
	two	rise to *demi-pointes*;
	three	hold.
2.	one	Step forward on the right foot, extending the left foot to *pointe tendue derrière*, arms rising to *croisé devant* position;
	two and three	hold.

*Measure 1 might better be considered as the preparation for the exercise, although Saint Léon numbers it as indicated here.

3.	one	*Elevé en attitude croisé;*
	two	hold;
	three	lower the left leg to *attitude demi-hauteur.*
4.	one	Close the left leg to fifth position back, *bras bas;*
	two	hold;
	three and	*demi-plié* and execute a *changement de pied* with one quarter turn to the right.
5.	one	Land in fifth position, left foot front, *corps droit;*
	two	rise to *demi-pointes;*
	three	hold.
6.–9.	one through *twelve*	Continue to the new side by stepping forward onto the left foot.
10.–17.	one through *twenty-four*	To reverse the exercise, proceed as above, but step backward in *croisé.* When raising the leg to *attitude devant,* raise both arms *haut,* then *à la seconde* as the leg lowers to *attitude demi-hauteur.*

ALLEGRO FROM THE PAST

The growing importance of steps of elevation is evident in the manuals of the nineteenth century. Again, changes in costume had encouraged more use of lively *allegro* movements. After the French Revolution beginning in 1789, elaborate fashions of the aristocracy—corsets, hooped skirts, wigs, heeled shoes—were shed along with the monarchy. Costumes for the stage reflected the simpler, less cumbersome social dress, allowing greater freedom for movement. One of the results in ballet was a gradual disappearance of the three distinct categories of dance styles—the noble or serious, the demi-character or lively, and the comic or rustic—in favor of a general virtuoso style. In 1820 Blasis observed that ". . . for a long time the noble and serious dance has been overlooked, in fact it is hard for us to conceive of dancing without gaiety."[26] Théleur remarked that by 1832 the grand noble and demi-character styles ". . . have been so blended with each other, that they now actually form but one, and the comic has latterly become almost obsolete."[27]

Even though all dancers could now "make use of all the movements and steps that the art offers," they were reminded that they should perform "their *temps d'abandon* accompanied by restraint and a pleasing dignity."[28] With this still-pertinent advice, we can consider the following *allegro* combinations, selected from the manuals for their appropriateness to contemporary intermediate technique.

TROIS CHANGEMENTS DE PIEDS, ÉCHAPPÉ, PIROUETTE SUR LE COU-DE-PIED, POSEZ DEVANT ET DE MÊME DE L'AUTRE JAMBE[29] (8 measures of 2/4)

Measure	Count	
		From fifth position, right foot front, *corps gauche, bras bas:*
	and	*demi-plié;*
1.	one, two	*changement, changement;*
2.	one	*changement;*

	two	*échappé sauté* with a quarter-turn right, *bras à la seconde*, landing in second position *demi-plié, corps droit*, left arm *arrondi*, right arm remaining *à la seconde*.
3.	*one, two*	*Pirouettes en dehors*[30] to the left, with the left foot placed
4.	*one*	*sur le cou-de-pied, bras bas*;
	two	close fifth position, left foot front, *corps droit*.
5.–8.	*one* through *eight*	Repeat the entire combination to the other side, finishing the *pirouettes* in fourth position, left foot front, legs straight, *corps de face, bras bas*.

A combination for *batterie*, called *brisés télémaque*, still seen in today's classrooms and listed in contemporary ballet dictionaries, no doubt was already a venerable exercise when Saint-Léon notated it in 1852. The combination possibly comes from the ballet, *Télémaque dans l'Ile de Calypso* (1790–1791), choreographed by Pierre Gardel, head ballet master for several decades at the Paris Opera.

Intermediate students are advised to begin with Saint-Leon's simple version before adding beats.

BRISÉS DE TÉLÉMAQUE SIMPLES[31] (8 measures of 3/4, moderato)

Measure	Count	
		From *pointe tendue croisé devant*, left foot front, *corps droit*, right arm *arrondi*, left arm *à la seconde*:
	and	prepare for an *assemblé derrière* by stepping diagonally forward onto the left leg in *fondu*, brush the right leg *à la seconde***demi-hauteur, bras bas*, and spring into the air, traveling to the right with the legs closing to fifth position *en l'air*, right foot back;
1.	*one*	alight from the *assemblé*, right foot back, *corps droit*;
	two	*changement de pieds* (without change of body direction);
	and	*sissonne simple* by bringing the legs to first position *en l'air* before
	three	landing on the left leg in *fondu*, right foot *sur le cou-de-pied derrière, corps droit*;
	and	execute an *assemblé dessus* traveling backward by brushing the right leg to fourth position *derrière demi-hauteur*, arms opening slightly forward (*demi-bras au public*), *corps en face*;
2.	*one*	land in fifth position, right foot front, *corps gauche, bras bas*;
	two	*changement de pieds* (without change of body direction);
	three	*sissonne simple* as above, landing in *fondu* on the right foot, left foot *sur le cou-de-pied derrière, corps gauche*.
3.–4.	*one* through *six*	Repeat the entire sequence to the other side.
5.–6.	*one* through *six*	Repeat the first side again, then finish the combination with:
7.	*one*	*assemblé derrière* traveling to the left;
	two	*changement*;

* Although the notation indicates second position, the leg would seem to brush slightly forward of second in order to maintain the direction of the body.

	three	*échappé sauté* to second position, *corps droit*, left arm *arrondi*, right arm *à la seconde;*
8.	*one and two*	*pirouette en dehors* to the left, left foot *sur le cou-de-pied, bras bas;*
	three	finish in fourth position, right leg front and straight, left foot *pointe tendue derrière, corps gauche,* arms slightly open *"au public."*

The same exercise with beats:

brisé dessus traveling sideward, *entrechat quatre, entrechat cinq, assemblé dessus battu* traveling backward (after the brush backward and while still in the air, bring the leg in to beat against the back of the front leg before closing to the front in fifth position), *entrechat quatre, entrechat cinq.*

Saint-Léon goes on to describe and notate a still more complex version of *brisés télémaque:*

brisé dessus traveling sideward, *entrechat six, entrechat sept* (like *entrechat six* except the landing is made on one foot, in this case on the front foot with the back foot raised *sur le cou-de-pied derrière*), *assemblé dessus battu* traveling backward, *entrechat six, entrechat sept.*

The following combination of *pas de bourrées* emphasizes quick footwork and a sideward bend or incline of the body, changing with each *pas de bourrée. Bras bas* are maintained throughout. The *pas de bourrées* do not finish in fifth position, but rather in *fondu* with the other leg extended *à la seconde demi-hauteur.* The accent is always on the *fondu* or completion of the step sequence (count *and* a **one,** *and* a **two,** etc.), resulting in a quick but gently swaying motion from side to side.

Saint-Léon does not give a title to this combination, but he employs the older and more descriptive terminology for *pas de bourrées:*

dessus et dessous: step over, step side, step under (now usually called *pas de bourrée dessus*)

dessous et dessus: step under, step side, step over (now, *pas de bourrée dessous*)

dessus: step over, step side, step over (now, *pas de bourrée devant*)

dessous: step under, step side, step under (now, *pas de bourrée derrière*)

In the following description, the older terminology of Saint-Léon will be used.

PAS DE BOURRÉES[32] (16 measures of 2/4)

measure	count	
		From fifth position, left foot front, *corps droit, bras bas:*
1.	*and* a **one**	*fondu* on the left leg and extend the right leg *à la seconde demi-hauteur, corps de face* and inclining slightly to the left, *pas de bourrée dessus et dessous,* changing the body to incline slightly to the right;
	and a **two**	*pas de bourrée dessous et dessus,* body inclining left;

2.	*and a one*	repeat all of the above;
	and a two	
3.–4	*one* through *four*	*pas de bourrées dessus* four times;
5.–8.	*one* through *eight*	repeat the entire sequence from the beginning.
9.–16	*one* through *sixteen*	Reverse the entire combination: *pas de bourrée dessous et dessus, dessus et dessous, dessous et dessus, dessus et dessous,* and *pas de bourrées dessous* four times. Repeat. Finish the final *pas de bourrée* in fifth position, right foot front, *corps gauche.*

Only one dance from the early nineteenth century survives in notated form, thus allowing its reconstruction. The survivor is *Gavotte de Vestris*, a dance for a couple, composed by the celebrated dancer-choreographer, Gaetano Vestris (1729-1808). The version notated and published by Théleur illustrates the dance qualities considered important: lively steps, springy elevation, and sparkling grace, set to a brisk musical score.

The opening phrase and first pattern of the Gavotte de Vestris *as depicted in* one version of notation by Théleur, Letters on Dancing. Collection of Laura Soave, *1831 edition.*

The step terminology used by Théleur occasionally differs from that used today. Therefore, in the following excerpt from the gavotte, movements that differ substantially will be described, then given their current name, followed by Théleur's term. Since arm movements were not shown in the notation, they are omitted here. The reader can devise *port de bras* in keeping with the style used in the previous combinations and shown in the accompanying illustrations, observing the general rule of opposition (left leg forward, right arm forward or high, etc.) and the preference for a well-rounded, slightly open shape for the arms.

EXCERPT FROM *GAVOTTE DE VESTRIS*[33] (16 measures of 2/4)

Measure	Count	
		From fifth position, right foot front, *corps de face:*
	and	*fondu* on the left leg and immediately slide the right foot forward (typically the notation does not specify the height of a raised leg; here a low *dégagé* level seems appropriate);
1.	*one*	small *jeté* forward onto the right foot;
	and	slide the left foot quickly into fifth position back;
	two	*assemblé dessus* (left foot finishing front);
2.	*one*	*changement de pieds*;
	two	*sissonne ouverte en avant*, landing on the right foot, left leg raised behind (probably a level of 45 degrees, *demi-hauteur*, is appropriate for this and the succeeding steps unless otherwise specified by the notation; it is possible that the raised leg is in *attitude* rather than lifted straight, another unclear point in the notation);
3.	*one*	spring backward onto the left foot, right leg raised behind (Théleur; *brisé* open);
	two	spring backward onto the right foot, left leg raised behind;
4.	*one*	spring onto both feet, landing fifth position *demi-plié*, left foot front (today: *assemblé dessus* without a brush to the side; Théleur: *brisé* closed);
	two	*sissonne simple devant*, landing on the right foot, left leg raised forward.
5.–8.	*one* through *eight*	Repeat the entire sequence to the other side, beginning with the *jeté* forward, but make the final *sissonne simple derrière*, landing on the right foot, left leg raised behind.
	and	Open the left leg to the side, pushing into the air off the right foot and traveling to the left;
9.	*one*	land in fifth position *demi-plié*, left foot back (today: *assemblé derrière*; Théleur: *brisé* closed);
	two	*sissonne simple derriere*, landing on the right foot, left leg raised behind;

10.	*one and two*	repeat Measure 9;
11.	*one*	spring backward onto the left foot, right leg raised behind (Theléur: *brisé* open);
	two	spring backward onto the right foot, left leg raised behind;
12.	*one*	spring into the air, bringing the legs together to land in fifth position *demi-plié*, left foot front (today: *assemblé dessus* without the brush to the side; Théleur: *brisé* closed);
	two	*sissonne simple derrière*, landing on the left foot, right leg raised behind;
13.–15.	*one* through *six*	repeat Measures 9–11 to the other side, but after the final spring backward, carry the right leg in an arc from back to front;
16.	*one*	place the right foot in fourth position *croisé en demi-pointe*;
	and	make a complete turn to the left on the left foot;
	two	finish on the left foot, right leg raised behind at hip level, body facing downstage left in *effacé*.

Illustrations of gently curved arms used in opposition to the well-stretched forward leg are typical of nineteenth-century style. Blasis, Code of Terpsichore, Plate VI, figure 2, and Plate VII, figure 1. Courtesy of Dance Horizon republication.

These are but a few of the challenging combinations from classes and choreography of the past. Although the lessons appear to have required great endurance, they seem to have offered chances for individualism and creativity as well:

> . . . to finish off the session, the class attacked the *temps terre à terre* and the *temps de vigueur*. The latter were sequences of *entrechats sous le corps* [without traveling], of *ronds de jambe*, *brisés*, of *entrechats à cinq*, of *fouettés sautés*, of *sissonnes* . . . and from them each dancer chose the one that seemed fitting to his inclinations. He gave particular attention to the task of perfecting it in order thus to create for himself a kind of dance and execution of it that were uniquely his.[34]

NOTES

1 August Bournonville, *My Theatre Life*, trans. Patricia N. McAndrew (Middletown, Conn.: Wesleyan, 1979), p. 405. Technical material from this master has been well treated in other texts, and therefore will not be repeated here. See Erik Bruhn and Lillian Moore, *Bournonville and Ballet Technique* (London: Adam and Charles Black, 1961); and the four volumes edited by Kirsten Ralov, *The Bournonville School* (New York and Basel: Audience Arts, a division of Marcel Dekker, Inc., 1979).

2 Available in a republication by Dover Publications, Inc., New York, 1968, translated into English by Mary Stewart Evans. Blasis' larger work, *Code of Terpsichore* (London, 1828), contains virtually identical technical material, but in addition has chapters on history, pantomime, composition of ballets and some scenarios, and social dance. It has been republished by Dance Horizons, New York. Hereafter, all references are to the 1820 volume.

3 Blasis, p. 19.

4 Adice's book, *Théorie de la Gymnastique de la Danse Théâtrale* (Paris, 1859), contains a fascinating chapter extolling the benefits of Blasis' rigorous class. For a translation of portions of that chapter ("An Account of the Principles of Our Traditions") see Selma Jeanne Cohen, *Dance as a Theatre Art* (New York: Dodd, Mead, 1974), pp. 71–77. The numbers quoted for barre exercises come from Adice's account.

5 Blasis, p. 19.

6 E. A. Théleur, *Letters on Dancing* (London, 1831), p. 96. Théleur possibly changed his name from Taylor. His book appeared in a second edition the very next year, and it is the 1832 edition hereafter referred to.

7 Blasis, p. 19.

8 Théleur, p. 58.

9 *Ibid.*, p. 96.

10 Blasis, p. 20.

11 Théleur, p. 96.

12 *Ibid.*, p. 55.

13 Misleadingly translated in the Dover edition as "running steps."

14 Translated from Adice, p. 76.

15 Théleur, pp. 29–30, 66. The timing indicated for the first sequence is based on the similar eighteenth-century *temps de courant*. See John Weaver, *A Small Treatise of Time and Cadence in Dancing* (London, 1706). The timing for the second sequence is an "educated guess," because Théleur provides no indication of meter for either sequence.

16 Adice, p. 76. Cohen, p. 75.

17 Théleur, pp. 38–39.

18 Saint-Léon, *La Sténochorégraphie ou Art d'écrire promptement la Danse* (Paris, 1852), p. 41, example 9. All musical references in the *allegro* combinations are to this treatise.

19 The exercise thus far resembles Cecchetti's *adage, Coupé et Fouetté, en avant et en arrière*. Indeed, he terms the steps forward and backward *coupés en avant* and *en arrière*. See Cyril W. Beaumont and Stanislas Idzikowski, *A Manual of the Theory and Practice of Classical Theatrical Dancing (Methode Cecchetti)* (1922; reprint ed., New York: Dover, Inc., 1975), p. 80.

20 Beaumont and Idzikowski, pp. 71–72.

21 Agrippina Vaganova, *Basic Principles of Classical Ballet* (Leningrad, 1934), Translation by Anatole Chujoy (New York: Dover, 1969), p. 132.

22 Saint-Léon, p. 45, example 13.

23 Cecchetti and Vaganova explain that during this leg movement (essentially a *grand rond de jambe en dehors*) the left arm is raised from *avant (arrondi)* to *haut* and thence *à la seconde*, while at the same time the right arm is raised from second to *haut*.

24 The four side-bend exercises were taught to the author by Dolores Mitrovich, who had been a student of Grassi's in Milan early in this century. She recalls that these exercises were invariably given as the first combinations in center floor each day.

25 Saint-Léon, p. 43, example 11.

26 Blasis, p. 56.

27 Théleur, p. 81.

28 Blasis, p. 57.

29 Saint-Léon, p. 48, example 18.

30 The directions and notation specify that four turns are to be made, but the intermediate student may attempt fewer.

31 Saint-Léon, p. 53, example 22.

32 *Ibid.*, p. 51, example 20.

33 Théleur, p. 72. For one interpretation of the entire dance notated in the Laban method, see the unpublished dissertation by Mary-Jane Evans Warner, "Gavottes and Bouquets: a Comparative Study in Changes in Dance Style Between 1700 and 1850" (Ohio State University, 1974). Available from University Microfilms International, Ann Arbor, Michigan.

34 Adice, p. 80. Cohen, p. 76.

EPILOGUE

Dance technique books look backward, not forward. That is, they describe what has been or is the case, not what will be. Even when changes are in the air, dance manuals seldom reflect them. One is reminded of the astounding technical innovation of dancing on point that was occurring on early nineteenth-century stages but was completely ignored or only casually mentioned in dance texts of the time (". . . this may be done on the ball of the foot or on the toes . . ."). So, too, has *Ballet: Beyond the Basics* tended to ignore contemporary choreographic trends that may eventually find reflection in ballet classrooms. Although some mention has been made of some relatively recent changes—the questioning of the benefits of *grands pliés* early in the lesson; the greater attention to larger, higher extensions; the elongation of a more streamlined ballet silhouette; and the use of systematic pre-barre warmups—no effort has been made to reflect the diversity of movement seen today on ballet stages; to catalogue the eclectic dance studies and backgrounds of many contemporary ballet dancers and teachers; to evaluate the various new approaches toward better body alignment, conceptions of mind-motor connections, and efforts to improve the efficiency and effectiveness of movement. The omission of references to these and other currents is not done from prejudice or disdain, but simply in recognition that no universal, fundamental shift has yet appeared in the ballet classroom format that signals a significant redirection of the technique.

Furthermore, this book is an intermediate text written essentially for adult, nonprofessional students and, thus, depicts a more modest movement range and classroom content than is the norm for advanced and professional dancers. If a fundamental change has recently occurred in the ballet classroom, it is with its occupants. No longer are they restricted to youngsters or to pre-professionals or to dance company members. Adult nonprofessional students now have the opportunity and encouragement to study an art form not from the "outside" as observers but from the "inside" as participants. Granted, participation may remain in the classroom and never reach the proscenium stage, but it is a common endeavor shared by amateur and professional alike. The classroom connection is an exciting, necessary link for all.

151

INDEX